CW01066690

LETTERS FROM

VOL. IV

received thru

Tuieta

published by

Portals of Light, Inc.

1993

Letters From Home: Vol. IV

Copyright © 1993 by Portals of Light, Inc.

ISBN 0-943365-19-8

Published by

Portals of Light, Inc.

P.O.Box 15621

Fort Wayne, IN 46885

Printed in the United States of America

FOREWORD

Over a period of several years the beloved ones of the Space Command have shared many messages and responded to many questions. Letters From Home Vol. I included messages received 1982 through 1984. These are grouped as: Religion; Governmental systems, ETs and UFOs; Brethren of the dark robes; Preparation for the period of tribulation; Relationships with ones of the unseen realms; Lift-off (date-time-place); Earth in the new day.

In Letters From Home Vol. II we "selected" a representation of messages received since 1984 regarding life on other planets; life on the ships; the seeding of planet Earth; their communication with us, and a simulated trip aboard a ship where the beloved ones respond to many of Earth mans questions.

In Letters From Home, Vol. III, we again "selected" a representation of messages received since 1984 regarding the energy infusion and the activation process; planet Earth and cosmic activity; the adult and child hu-man; the animal kingdom; tools for assisting ourselves; helping others; and reaching our own potential.

This present volume is a companion to Vol. III, and with the assistance of beloved Sarna, we have added certain introductory headings/comments/questions in order to help in the flow of material. Also we have "edited" certain portions of some of the messages. However, the channeled material that is included is exactly as received and there has been no attempt to alter the thought or feeling intent that was sent forth.

Future volumes will include such things as extensive teachings they have shared that will help us to, learn - understand - KNOW.

i

I, Tuieta, am greatly honored to be the means by which these thoughts can be shared with my fellow travelers on planet Earth. The channeled messages came as words/thoughts that were impressed upon my conscious mind by the beloved ones who are among our many unseen brothers, sisters, teachers, guides, friends. I make no claim regarding this material except to say I was used as an instrument that this TRUTH might be shared with mankind.

Please keep in mind the degree of purity of these messages is dependent upon the level of evolvement of myself, as the channel, at the time they were received.

As you read of these books may you be filled with the love, the joy, the peace, the brotherhood that I felt from the beloved ones as each message was shared through me, and may you glean from them that which will assist you in your preparation for the Day of the Golden Son.

Tuieta and David

CONTENTS

INTRODUCTION

Good evening. Blessings in the Light of the Most Radiant One. I am Monka. I hold a bonding with Earth and her inhabitants which covers multiple life times for each of you. I have been the representative of you and your planet Earth in the councils and tribunals, and I shall continue to be the voice which speaks on behalf of you at these meetings until the point is reached when you can and do stand as your own representatives within the councils and tribunals. My love for all of you goes far beyond that which can be expressed in words. I hold all of you close to my heart.

We have asked this one through which we speak to compile the materials which we have shared with her into specific categories or topics. Most of these topics have been initiated by you through your questions and shared thoughts. In this small volume we ask to share thoughts with you concerning that which is about you on or about your planet which impacts upon you. We ask you to see you are in the process of change. You call this tribulation.

This change shall grow in momentum until Earth, as you acknowledge it, is not there, but rather new facets of the Earth Mother present themselves for your exploration. New experiences await you; experiences which have not been heretofore available because of the density carried by the corporeal man.

But before entering the New Day, let us in retrospect observe those institutions which have held you bound, which have programmed your thinking into compliance. Let us see that which has donned the garment of Savior as it truly is, a philosophy which seeks to gain from you for its own elevation in the material realm.

What is your government? What component lies quietly within and without it to control you? What is the concept behind one world government and how has that been manipulated to be one world under one control for one benefit? Do the ET's of your dimension play a part in this? If so, what is their part?

And lastly, is there hope? Is there a potential for a new earth, cleansed and ready for new beings? Where will you go during this process? How will you get there? Is there anyone in the Cosmos who cares and sees you as the Divine beings you are? These are some of the thoughts we would share with you in this small volume.

Begin your readying with a sharp sense of discernment. Accept truth as it presents itself to you. Know we, of the Ashtar Command, have enfolded this small volume in love. May you feel that love and caring as you partake of our words. I am Monka, a most humble servant of the Radiant One.

RELIGION

Even as Commander Monka closes his shared thoughts, so it is that each is bathed in love, in wisdom, in Truth. I am Sarna. I shall be your coordinator during your journey of this small volume. I am Tuieta's companion and link with the Ashtar Command. I hold the privilege of maintaining a clear communicative link with her for the Command for all communications.

The first topic of our discussion is the one of earth religions. The Lord Sananda, Lord Dionus, Commanders Hatonn, Jokhym and Soltec as well as Commander Monka and I will share thoughts and answer questions on this topic. Commander Hatonn is the first to answer questions.

How has the present day Christian Church gone so far afield?

HATONN Greetings, my brothers, my sisters. ...This question has been with me for a time too, my sister. Indeed, this is a question that has puzzled many of us on this plane. In actuality, that which was taught by Jesus Sananda has been used by man of man's purpose. And though there are ones, such as you and you and you, who have followed of these teachings in your early life, there has been a question within your being of these. As your various churches have come forth, they have picked specific passages, specific portions of the written word. And indeed, they have made these gospel, gospel to the point that they did not recognize the word itself.

As you look back through your history since our beloved one walked with you, there have been many struggles upon your earthly plane. And there have been ones that

3

have sought to elevate themselves in any way that was possible. And indeed, they have taken the teachings, or shall I say, they have used or abused the teachings that were shared so freely, to elevate themselves as individuals.

I would give you this example: As we sit and we speak brother with brother, and brother with sister, this is a comfortable relationship that we enjoy and we share. And yet, do you recognize how many of your city, of your state, of your country that would have you burned at the stake for such a gathering? Does this help you to understand? Man has taken of the gifts of the treasures that have been shared, that are his Divine inheritance, and these have been buried by these dark ones, these dark ones that have sought to elevate themselves. And so it is that the gifts that are Earth man's have been lost, have been buried.

I would add here, a word, a note that has caused great concern, and I would share of my concern with you this hour. There are many denominations, or religions, churches, call them what you will upon your Earth at this time. Many of these have been infiltrated by the brothers of darkness as an attempt to bind man to specific thoughts, to specific ways, and close his eye to that which is coming, to that which is his right and his inheritance. This has been used by the brothers of darkness to bind man to worship other men, to be bound in the thinking that there would be no free thought, that there would be no exchange of ideas. But rather man, Earth man, would be a robot that would follow as another leads them. The Divine Creator asks this of no man, but it is asked of each man that he take to his altar that which he receives that only the truth of the Divine Principle might abide with him...

Our religions have taught us certain things about love, and it is coming into our awareness that maybe that is not the real love that there is. Can you help us understand why this type of religion, this type of teaching, was given to us then, seeing that it does not seem to fit any

4

more with our understanding of the way the Divine Creator works?

HATONN You would speak of that which is the evolutionary process of the conscious thinking entity that is known as Earth man kind. Long ago man understood that unconditional love was his. It is demonstrated by a state of being, to Be. There are no limitations. There are no parameters that are placed there.

However, look at the way you would raise your small children, those ones that have been entrusted to you. When first they learn to crawl you limit their space that they would not harm themselves. This limitation may be by a fenced-in area, it might be by your immediate supervision. But then they learn to walk. Hence, you allow them more space. But as they would begin to walk, you do not let them cross the busy street alone, but you would hold their hand, for initially they would not understand your "stop, look, and listen". It is only later that they would learn this, and then they would be able to cross the street.

The point that I am making is, that which is shared is shared as the collective consciousness will tolerate the sharing. There have been that which has been considered the clergy of your religions, of your Christianity, and others. They have done that which to them is truth at that hour, and that was what man's collective consciousness would allow, which he would allow brought forth. You are going into a shift in your own collective consciousness, that which is the consciousness of human on planet Earth. You are, if you can visualize this, pebbles that are being placed on the heap that have bumps and edges, and you are causing a shaking in the collective consciousness -- you of this group, you of that group, you of other groups, other workers of the Light about the planet. As you do this, then you are helping, assisting, awakening the awareness of ones on your planet to come into that which is a state of being.

There are many steps that must be taken, just as your

5

infant must crawl before it can walk. There are steps of non-judgment, of a minimum of expectations of others, of allowing the other to be all they can be, of accepting them where they are, and of accepting yourself in the same manner.

These are but a few of the thoughts that would go into bringing forth the concept, the understanding of unconditional love. For love is. You are, on your planet, beginning to feel the impact of those two words. You are altering the consciousness of your planet by this. The reason that you can do this is because you have come from places, states of consciousness, in which you experienced this balance and attunement. Hence, you have come here to demonstrate it to others. Some of you get a little tangled in the process, but the motive is pure, I assure you...

What about the idea that the life of Jesus was a holograph that was inserted into our history by ETs?

JOKHYM Greetings in the Light of the Radiant One. ...There are those who have come from other spheres and they have said that the whole basis of your christian religion is a holograph that they had sent forth. What does your heart tell you? What does your heart tell you? What better way to cause an uncertainty in a consciousness than to take away the one pillar which has stood for many eons on your time? What better way? Your religions upon your plane have caused enough problems without any external influence. They do not need that kind of help.

I speak from the Totality of my Being when I say, ones have walked your plane and they are avatars, for they are ones who have come on particular missions, to share portions of cosmic truths. Each has been recognized in his own way, in the area of your planet and at the period of evolution when they have entered. What has caused the sadness within our hearts is that the collective consciousness of man has not seen the similarity in the teachings of the avatars, but they have seen only the differences.

This one whom you call the Christ, the Master Jesus, though he is not historically documented on your planet, according to some thinking, walked the plane of planet Earth. He experienced as any man experienced at that point in your own cycle. He was one who entered into the Christed state while he was on your planet. The divine portion, his soul, knew this was possible for him and hence he accepted this assignment, if you will, this job, this whatever you would call it. Our concern is when you say, "He is The Christ." For you know The Christ is a station within the Divine Totality, and there are ones beside the Master Jesus who have attained this station.

But I did not choose to enter into a theological discussion at this point. I merely would make the point that this Great One, this Being, has entered upon your plane and has walked of your plane. He was not a holograph. He is not a holograph. But indeed as there were ones before him, so he walked also.

Religion and the belief in the Source, One Source has been the strength of all civilizations. The civilizations upon your plane who have chosen to deny this Source or have attempted to manipulate mans connection with the Source have been the civilizations who have gone down, who are no longer in function. So do not be concerned. That belief system within the heart of the collective consciousness of Earth Man kind is quite strong. Though, this one whom is the Source of Being, may be called by many different names, and the one who is the son may be called by even many more, I assure you it is all in operation and doing well.

With the great conflicts of the religions through the centuries, I just feel its been a system of control.

JOKHYM We can take no credit for this. This is it exactly, it has been a system of a control. But this control has been set about by the consciousness that is man. It has not been instigated by that which is an exterior motive. It has been that which has been mans desire to control man. It is a power game. And if you have power over this one, then truly you are greater than this one. Is that not so? ("Yes.") And this has been going on through the ages. It has been going on before your time of Moses, or that which is the record of the beginning of creation.

Your religions, that which were the teachings of the one that is known as the Master Jesus, the one that is known as the Buddha, all of these ones, the teachings were, are and will be -- did I cover all of your tenses -- to be all you can be and be the God within you. It is only when you give your power to another -- and see power cannot be taken, power can only be given -- and when you would give your power to another and feel that you must go through them as the door, then it is that truly you have difficulty. But part of this you recognize is an evolutionary process. It is your own growth process.

Two thousand years ago on your calendar, the Master Jesus said to you that all he did you can do to. It has only taken you two thousand years to begin to understand what this meant, huh? Seeds are planted by these ones and then they will grow and they will flourish and they will bring forth a beautiful flower when you are ready to be that blossom...

Could you discuss the role of the Bible relative to today?

SARNA That which is known as your Holy Book is indeed one which is filled with great truth. However, this truth was recorded by that which is called mortal man. And mortal man, as he has recorded this and as he has taken those recordings and he has copied them, has oft times put an individual interpretation upon that which was originally given. Please understand, this was not done intentionally to mislead anyone. It was done in that which is a faith in what was being done. This is what happened originally.

However, there were ones who felt they had the right to control others. And so, they put in slight alterations and took out certain portions which were to be contained in this Holy Writing. This was done to control. Keep in mind, the original recordings are available on your planet at this time. However, that which is the works known as your Holy Book must be read with great discernment, and there are portions which you must recognize are a story which was told, which was given as an explanation for an act for people who had an understanding at that point, primarily that which is your Old Testament. It is not to be said that ones were giving an inaccuracy; they were merely telling a story, because the people at that time could not understand except by a story. And the recordings are in the language of the understanding of the peoples at that point.

So through your ages, not only have you had additions and omissions within the Holy Works, but you have also had those who have added the thought as to the meaning of some of the words which were used. Many of your present day religions have come as a result of ones putting their interpretation on specific meanings, and they are sure they are right. And their sureness has assisted others in their growth. However, there are inaccuracies, there are myths, there are great truths within this book, and they are all mixed together. Truly it is an assignment for a most learned and a most patient and wise one to go through their discernment process with this.

May I suggest, as you would read this book, as you would read all books, you would hold them in your hand and you would ask that you would receive only truth. You will find that some of the passages within this great book will become suddenly very clear to you as you do this. Just as you will find as you read other books, you will have a clarity and an understanding.

SARNA (continues) ...There are those written words within your book, your Holy Book, that have been taken as an absolute gospel, and yet these words have been changed ever so slightly that the total meaning has been altered.

I will give you an example. That which is the word that is called fear, you recognize this in your Holy Book. If you would go to that which were the original writings, long ago, that were given from ones of other dimensions, you will find in most instances, in that which is your old testament, where the word fear is used, the word love was intended. Has this not altered meaning?

There are books that are available that are truly channeled works, i.e., A Course In Miracles. Are these to help us clarify what was already written?

SARNA All works come forth to assist you. It is how you use this assistance that gets to be the problem. So if you read all things desiring truth, and hold the volume in your hands when you ask this, you will find you will receive the greatest truth. That which you call A Course In Miracles has opened the door and sent many forth on a wondrous path of self discovery and understanding of their connection with the Source of their Being.

Is there a specific bible that you would recommend?

SARNA No. Indeed, much of that which you know as your Bible has been greatly adulterated, and there is much that has been lost, for man has chosen to delete and to insert to suit of his own purposes. Yet, I would say to you that that which follows closely, most closely, that which is known to you as your King James version which follows most closely the vibrational pattern of your early Atlantean language would help to stimulate certain specific centers within your brain to awaken...

In the Bible when they talk about the ending of the times, and they say "Woe be to those who have children during this period." Is that truth? If I desire children, should I say, "No, I do not want children at this time because I don't want to see my children suffer with the cleansing of the Earth and whatever will come to pass," and I should choose not to experience that?

JOKHYM I shall not respond to the question, but what I will respond to is the desire to bring forth another. What is your intent? In the quietness of your being, as you would sit in the quietness of your being, ask. Is there one you have contracted with to work on a form to bring forth that another being might incarnate? If there is one, then do you ask in peace that you be the vessel that you would finish this? Then do not worry.

That which is called your book of Revelations was given to a most beautiful one and was given in pictures that had meaning for this one. The mystery has been the interpretation by all ones who would read it. Each of you must listen within your heart what you must do. For you may find as you read of the great book there will be many places that would say to you to have of a child and to not have of a child. But it is only you within your heart that knows what your role is. And there is in that which is not too distant a day many of you that would be of ones to bring forth children, would find you have communication with this one prior to it coming. What greater gift could there be than for you to know and recall the one that would enter through you? Search that which is beyond the dimension for your answer.

Could you speak about the Ark of the Covenant, the energies that are contained within it, and if these are now available to us?

SARNA There is truth that those energies that were once contained in a specific form are now available upon your planet for many ones. Indeed, these energy patterns have been brought to your planet by specific ones, because of your evolutionary status at this time of your cyclic change.

Man has gone from the worship of many to the worship of one, recognizing there is but one God, one Total. There are many portions to this Total. Ones upon your planet at this evolutionary period of your cycle are now sufficiently tuned that these energies might be shared throughout the planet system. As you, man upon the planet Earth, comes into the fullness of that which you are, you shall be each initiated into the Holy service that you would receive of these energies "In toto" according to your ability to receive.

You have been told on many occasions that the mysteries which have been locked away are coming into a focus, are coming into your own understanding. You have evolved that can accept these in the truth which they are that you no longer have the need to misuse or abuse the sacred gifts or the precious rites. Thus it is that you are the Covenant, you are the Holy Grail for you hold within you all of the secrets, all of the mysteries, all of the perfection, for you are the manifestation upon your plane. Each of you are mighty vessels. Each of you are Gods within your own totality. It is only as you evolve into this that you come into the recognition of the sacred trust that has been placed within you.

Could you tell us anything about Judas?

HATONN ...There has been one that has been condemned, not only of his life time but for all eternity, that he would be one that would be looked upon most unfavorably by Earth man kind because of his act, one particular act when he was on planet Earth. I am referring to the disciple that was known to you as Judas. This man, this individual, this thought form has been condemned through all eternity, according to you of Earth, for his act. And yet his act was a significant part to play out the final drama that had to be played. This one was very close to the one that you knew as Jesus. There was a great love and a great bond between them. And yet man has said he denied the Savior, he sold the Savior. In fact this day in your language when one betrays a trust he is called a "Judas". And yet you or none that walk the face of Mother Earth know what it was that this one that was known to you as Judas contracted to do, and what he did knowing that he would be despised by his brothers and sisters over many eons.

How do the predictions of the Space Brothers relate to bible prophecy? Can any definite references be offered?

MONKA That which we share with you Eartheans in no way is a contradiction to what is said in your bible, particularly your Book of Revelations. However, I would say the original truths that were intended to be presented in this most holy book have been adulterated so that it should, or would be, difficult for many to see how that which is stated in your bible and which we state are one and the same.

What of the relationship of the "born again Christian" and those which are known as Light workers, and the interaction that they have?

MONKA Blessings in the Light of the Radiant One. ...I presume as you speak of the "born again Christian", you are speaking of this one that has realized within your religious dogma and confines that they are a child, or a creation, or a manifestation of the Perfect Principle which is known to you as God the Father. These ones, as you would say, have accepted the one that is known to us as Jesus Sananda as their savior. This brings forth a great measure of confusion, just by these statements that I have said.

Our beloved Commander-in-Chief as he walked with

you came to walk, to teach, to be the perfect example of that which you are capable of. However, your established religions have taken that which he would teach, which he would share, which he would show, and it has been greatly adulterated. And he has been set upon a pedestal to be worshipped and idolized. He asks of all men of all man kind to worship him not, but to walk with him as a brother. For he has come, he came, and he will come again as the Elder Brother to walk with you, to show you how you might realize that which you truly are.

Light workers are legions of volunteers, those that are awakening, have questioned of the established dogma of organized religion. They have questioned many of the thoughts that were brought forth in a dogmatic fashion that were to be accepted in totality with no question. As ones on the physical plane have had communication with those of the higher dimensions, as ancient writings have been brought forth and revealed, it has been shown that there has been an adulteration to that which our beloved Commander-in-Chief attempted to teach to you of Earth.

At this time, we and all ones that are working with Earth under the Great Brotherhood are attempting to help each one soul portion on the Earth plane that would make the choice to come forth in the Light, in the realization that they are of the Divine Creation, that they have within them all that is possible on all dominions if they would grow, if they would evolve into that state or dimension.

You of your western sector of your planet follow of the one that is known to you as Jesus the Christ. In other portions there is Buddha, there is Mohammed. There are still others that are followed. Recognize that each one of these came forth with specific portions of teachings. You of Earth have taken the teachings of one specific Master, and you have made these the absolute Law. In this manner, the mysteries will never come to you for you have only one portion.

In the days to come, you will recognize that each great and glorious one that came forth brought with them specific lessons, specific teachings that Earth man was ready for at that point in his evolution. And so as these teachings come together and you look at them as part of a total picture so shall you then begin to see the truth of some of that which is known to you as the great and the mighty mysteries.

Will you please speak to the change in the thinking process that we are going through between the New Age thinking and the thinking that has been on Earth for a couple thousand years by many of the churches, that is that Jesus is the only Son of God?

DIONUS Salutations, Eartheans. ...Initially may I say, there is no new age or new movement. There is merely that which is a cycle that is coming into its infancy. Those of you upon your planet that are looking toward the beginning of another cycle are terming yourselves to be New Age. For indeed it is a new age for you, this one that is coming forth. But in truth, that which is shared with you, that which you feel within your heart cell is as old as creation itself. Most ones upon your planet see conflict as a negative tool. For indeed, in most cases it brings two opposing forces directly head to head. But I would ask of you, can this not also bring about a great good? For as two opposing thought forms would come together, they would create questioning within the minds eye of both sides of the factions.

Recognize that which is known to you as your orthodox religion has served and does serve a very valuable purpose. The teachings that have come forth from your orthodox religions has allowed you to be where you are in your evolution. For had it not been for these thoughts then the next steps would not be ready.

That one that is known to you as the Master Jesus issued in a specific age, the age of the fisherman. Was not the symbol of these early ones the fish? For he put out thoughts. He fished that you, dear fishes, could come toward that which he shared. Many of the teachings that he shared when he was upon your planet in physical form were teachings that are beginning to come into your awareness at this time. Why? Because you were not ready for them when he shared them.

He spoke. He taught. He was an example to usher in a new age, an age of One God, of brotherhood. That was a totally new concept at the time when he came to Earth. But even as he shared these thoughts, he also shared thoughts to prepare you to step into the next cycle or age as you would call it. As he spoke of brotherhood was not that given as a speech, as a thought form for you this day in acceptance of others?

This one that was known to you as the Master Jesus never, never claimed he was the only Son of the Lord God of Totality. That right was written in by ones upon your planet. He came to be an example. But in order for you to follow the example that he gave to you, you had to go through this period of that which you would call your orthodox religions. All is of its purpose and all is of Divine Order. It is now that ones begin to look, begin to question, and old writings are coming into ones awareness to help you to understand and to expand upon the teachings that the beloved Master Jesus shared when he was upon your planet.

This confrontation that many of you see, and that you have experienced, and you will experience in greater severity, is one of a sorting, is one of a teaching, is a growth process. Is not that delightful? Is not that wonderful? And there is a lesson in this for each one -- Be. Allow each one his own place that he might be. Recognize that as there are ten million walking side by side each one is on a different path. And one cannot step over to walk the path of his brother without being accountable for his brother. Be. Walk your own path in peace, in truth, in harmony, and allow your brother to do the same.

That is a lesson that many of your, shall we say "New Age thinkers" have difficulty accepting, for in their enthusiasm and their realization of who they are, they would desire most truly and honestly to share this with all others. But recognize not all others are ready for the truth that is your truth. You must allow each one their own truth even as you would be allowed your own.

Could you please bring forth from the records one of the conversations of Jesus with his disciples concerning the period that we are in now?

HATONN Indeed, beloved Light, I shall share with you of a discourse that was given by that one that was known to you as Jesus to those ones that were his followers as they journeyed about the hills to the smaller cities in which the Word was shared. This was spoken shortly before the Last Supper or that time which you know as the Last Supper, in which this Beloved One was trying most desperately, most earnestly, to awaken these ones that were committed to bring forth the Word.

He spoke to them of why he had come to Earth. He spoke to them of how he came to Earth, and what his purpose was. He spoke of ushering in a new era. He spoke of the new commandment that he had given to them. That this was his purpose for coming. They nodded, but they truly did not understand what he was saying.

And he spoke of what they must do at that hour, at that time. And his vision was a far seeing vision. And he saw what would happen, of what was planned to happen. And he told them as he would leave of them in that form that he would leave with them a great power and a great gift, and that which they said and that which they did, and that which they held most closely to their hearts would be felt o'er eons on planet Earth.

He spoke of how man would evolve. And man would

17

come to realize that he was not male or female, but that he was both. And up until the period in which he walked this Earth that which is known as the male portion of man had been dominant, and had made slaves and servants of the female. And he had come to usher in an age, a period of recognizing that there was need for each, and that within the two components, the male and the female, that there must be balance, there must be harmony.

He spoke of the struggles that you have experienced, that were the direct result of his teachings. And he spoke of this age, this time in which you are entering, in which there would be an equality of your positive and your negative. That as you love yourself, as you love your brother so do you love all of creation, for you have reached a state to be one with creation. There is an equality in creation. He spoke of the strengths that each brings upon this planet. He spoke of the gentleness of the woman, and the great gift that she has. And he spoke to these ones, these rough unpolished gems, of the gentleness. And he asked of them to nurture within their own heart that which was the love that his mother exemplified.

He spoke of the change that was to come. And he spoke of the desire this change would be a beautiful and a peaceful one, that man on Earth would meld into that which he could be. He spoke of this as the Plan for Earth, though his eye gazed about and his eye did not see Earth man that would step into this new awareness without a struggle. He spoke to them of peace, and of joy, in commitment, in contentment.

And he said to them their would be a day on Earth that all men would walk as brothers, and none would lift sword against another. And he spoke to them of wives, of mothers, of sisters not being afraid, of having no fear for they would be recognized for their true worth. They would be recognized for all the beauty that they are. They would no longer be sold or bartered or swapped for other goods, but they would be equal upon this planet with that which is known as the man kind. He spoke of love. He spoke of peace.

And these ones though their souls knew very well of what he spoke, their minds listened in absolute wonder for they had great difficulty comprehending the morrow, much less two thousand years, two thousand fifty years later. They listened as with many of the lessons that he shared with them, they did not at that time fully comprehend what he was saying to them. And they asked him, "Master, will you come back, and will you be here with us?" And he told them that he would never really leave them. And yes, he would walk with them. And they drew great comfort from this. And so it is, they proclaimed to all ones that he would return, that he would come to walk with them. And this teaching has gone forth for these hundreds of years.

But somehow the part of the lesson where he spoke of brotherhood, where he spoke of love, and he spoke of at-one-ment -- which is to raise your vibratory rate to a higher state of consciousness -- this was omitted. This was not heard. But what was heard was he would return. And in their mind's eye they heard this, and they thought he will perform, he will do all of the wondrous things he has done now, and he will do even more. And so, over this period of time, ones continually wait for his return. Yes, ones continually wait, and they sit with their hands folded most patiently waiting, little recognizing that they have their part which they must do in order for him to return.

The way that man of Earth goes into this new state of awareness, this new consciousness is of his own choice. For he is the one that has created the unbalanced ledger that must be balanced. This he has done by his own choice. The method of the evolution has been left to him; but he will evolve. He will awaken into an equality and a oneness with all of creation.

This the Master Jesus spoke of in simple terms with those ones that followed with him. This the Master Jesus tried to convey. And when he would feel of the confusion, and he could read within their eyes that they did not truly understand what he was speaking to them, he would retreat into a place of solitude that he might be in communion with his Father who had sent him unto this plane. And he would say to Him, "My Father, they do not understand. They do not understand. What can I do? What can I do to help them understand that which they must do, that which they have come to do?" And a great Light would flood his being and within him would come the words, "BE STILL. BE STILL. BY MYNE HAND YOU HAVE COME. AND BY MYNE HAND ALL IS MADE MANIFEST."

Wasn't Jesus a martyr?

JOKHYM He has been seen that way by many ones upon your planet. He had no intent to be a martyr. He came to demonstrate a lesson. He came to build on that which has been given by ones of the great teachers that came before him. He added another piece to the puzzle and it is that the teachings that he would share are part of the teachings that have been shared such as by the Buddha, Zoroaster and some of the others.

This one that came, came to show you what you are. Because it was not until this time that you were ready to think about it -- recognizing full well as he did this, knowing full well that there would be a cycle that would go through in which you would not vaguely understand what he was trying to tell you. And that what he said it would take many thousands of years before there would begin to be a realization of what he meant. But because there is no time, that thousands of years is but a blink of the eye.

And what is the form? It is a vehicle to use within your dimension. If you recognize that you are eternal, you are ready to lay down the form at any moment for it is only a tool and it is a tool that limits you to your dimension. Would you choose to be limited to the dimension that you are in?

Or, would you choose to be that which is one which would travel of all the dimensions? You have your choice. But his was a lesson he would share with you knowing full well that it would take two thousand years for this awareness to come.

When he spoke, most oft he spoke as that which was the Christed station, the son of God, as <u>one</u> of the sons of God, the Christos. He did not speak as the man. The interpretation by many ones as far as your Bible is concerned, this Holy Writ, is he spoke as that which was the individual. He spoke as that which was the station. And that has been the mystery for Earth man kind...

Who is the original creator, if not Jesus? This thought presupposes the trinity of the Godhead.

DIONUS There is but one Creator and that is the Lord of Totality, the Supreme Source from whence all comes, who in the beginning was and is, and always shall be. And all comes forth from that which is the Supreme Source, the Omnipotent Source, the Omnipotent Force that sends forth the thought form that brings into manifestation that which you know as creation, that which you know as God.

Will the one that we knew as Jesus, that we know as Sananda be returning to Earth in the physical form as stated in the book of Revelations?

MONKA ...As you think about, as you ponder of the return of this one that is known to you as Jesus, there are several factors that are involved in this return. One, each of you within your own total entity is a christ. Now this is something that is not particularly palatable to your way of thinking, for you have received a beautiful indoctrination to the contrary. Just as, the Beloved One has been quoted to say that he died for your sins. And he has said to you that he doesn't need your sins, they're yours alone.

You must recognize that this one that was known to you as Jesus spoke of many things, he spoke of them not as Jesus the man, but he spoke of them as that One which is the Christed Station. The interpretation by many ones of Earth has been that, "Jesus said this...," or "Jesus said that...." Jesus the physical form was the vehicle through which the Christ spoke and worked. This vehicle had been attuned to such a degree that it was in absolute harmony with the Christed energies. This is where most of you of Earth have difficulty. Though you have this same seed, this same ability within you, you are not, you have not, you have chosen not -- and here I underline the word chosen -- you have chosen not to attune yourselves to the point that the dear one known to you as Jesus did. Thus, that which is known as the Christ within your being does not find as easy access through you as it did through him.

And so as it was spoken of that he would return to Earth, he would walk of Earth, this is so. The Christ does walk of Earth. He walks within each of you. That which is the Christed walks within each of you. And the Beloved One who has grown beyond the proportion of Jesus, who is the composite of the total energies of the Christed station, who has achieved this dimension, this growth because of the life of the one that was known to you as Jesus, this one that we speak of as Sananda, our beloved leader, our guide, our Commander-in-Chief.

Yes, he shall be on Earth. He shall be seen on Earth, just as he has been seen on Earth, and just as he has walked on Earth. But may I offer a thought for your consideration? Unless your eyes are opened and you are attuned, you will not see him. You must look for him, and as you look for him so will he reveal himself to you...

* * * * *

SANANDA Honi Honi Honi Would ye hear that which I would give? Would ye receive that which I have cum to bring? For it is I have spoken to thee of many things and I

22

have spoken to thee in many ways. And some of ye have heard of that which I have said. And some of ye have felt of my touch as I did approach thee. And it is now I do call to thee to hear, hear well that which ye have been given, and be ye as one to take to thy heart that which ye have been given. For the hour is cum, and ye ones who would choose not to hear of the hour but would choose to walk thy state in darkness, so be it, that is thy choice, and ye shall be as ones accountable for thy choice.

But ye ones who would choose to walk of the Light, who would follow after me, so be it, I shall not fail thee. For kno ye are kno-n to me, and kno ye are dear unto myne heart. For I shall give to thee the strength and the succor that ye need in this thyne hour of tribulation. For thy hour of tribulation is with thee, and thy hour of testing is upon thee.

And it is that ye shall not convert these ones who chuz (choose) not to hear, for it is they have of their own choice and their own hearing. And if they chuz not to hear that which we would speak, then so be it. Let them go forth that they might be free, that they might be as ones accountable for their own.

But, ye ones who do receive, who do follow of me, I say gather ye close and lend of thyne ear. For it is that I do cum to give to thee that portion you have need of.

Be ye as ones to kno the hour has cum when a great storm shall cum across the land, and the winds shall howl and they shall moan, and there shall be great waters. And that which was below the waters shall be above. And that which is above the waters shall go below. For the hour has cum that there shall be a great unsettling of the land, and as the land is unsettled so shall there be a sorting.

And ye ones who would hear of that which I do say shall be taken into that place which is kno-n as my safe place. For not one hair of thy head shall be touched. For did I not say to thee I would care for thee? Did I not say that I would look after thee? It be so, it be so. For myne Father has

23

sent me into the land that I might nourish, that I might guide, that I might watch over ye ones of our flock. Kno ye that naught that is of the tribulation shall abide with thee. But, ye shall shed of this as the snake does shed of its skin. And as ye do shed of thy tribulation so shall ye be as one to gro in thy skin of Light. And so shall thy Light be greater. And so shall it be seen.

I am thyne elder brother who does speak. I am kno-n of many names. I am Esu within myne Father's house. I am Sananda to ye ones who do walk of the New Day. And to ye ones whose eye is cast behind I am kno-n as Jesus. But, I say to each I am the Christos, I am the Christos. Kno as ye receive of me so are ye blest in thy receiving. And as ye do walk with thy hand placed in myne so are ye guided by the Divine Light.

I have cum to claim thee O'Brethren, I have cum to claim ye. And I do send ones about the land to collect thee, that none shall be lost.

Now ones shall say, "He speaks not thru this one." Or, "He speaks not thru that ones pen." So be it, if this is as they would think. But I say to them, the day shall fall upon their head when they shall recognize of these ones I have sent unto them. For I have sent ones across the land that each might hear of myne word, that each might receive. And these ones do cum as my priests, as myne priestesses. They do cum as myne handmaidens and myne man servants. And they do cum with myne authority. And they speak not as the voice which is their own, but they do speak that which I do put within their mouth. Receive ye and kno ye receive of myne word. Receive ye and kno they do speak with myne authority.
Now it is I am thyne elder brother, I am the Christos.
Selah Selah Selah
Om ni di eno cum eta

* * * * *

24

Is there any value in observing Lent?

MONKA This period that you know as Lent has been well documented within your ecclesiastical circles. This I would say, this period of abstinence, this period of recognition, does not have to be in a particular period in your calendar, but this is as individual as there are individuals that walk the face of Mother Earth.

In early times, and here I speak of church times, this period that is known to you as Lent was used as a period to bring the populous under control. This was used as a time to remind these ones that do follow, that they are not worthy, that they need to be cleansed out, that they are self indulgent, that they are selfish. And this also was used as opportunity for the ones of the church to be beautifully pious, and to walk about with their halos very straight.

This period belongs to each of you as you are ready to observe it, but it cannot be dictated to you for that which is within your heart is known to you alone. Yes, it is good for ones to fast. It is good for you to recognize that you have been over indulgent, and to modify your indulgence. But as you bring yourself into attunement and harmony with all of the Creative Process, then there is no need for this period that you call Lent, for you will be in such an attunement and at-one-ment that these areas shall be erased from you.

As that which is known as your formal religion crumbles and leaves of this plane to allow each one to come forth in their own right, to listen to the leaders, to those that are wiser, who have studied of the Law, who have lived in the attunement, then such specific outward recognitions and manifestations shall not be necessary.

Could you tell us about the Wesak Festival?

MONKA This is at the time of the first full moon in June, and is a time that the Buddha comes to bless and mingle energies with the Christed One that the Light of the Christed station is shared evenly throughout all of Earth for the remainder of the year. This is a time that the energies of love and wisdom mingle in truth, that are sipped by all ones of all dimensions that strive for the upliftment of ones of Earth...

And the Festival of Love?

SARNA   Just as at the Wesak Festival that the Buddha shares the cup with the Christed One, and in turn all ones are allowed the opportunity to drink of the cup of at-one-ment, so it is that the Festival of Love is an initiatory step for those who would drink of the cup to allow them to come into their state of at-one-ment, to come into their Christed state. It is at the time of the Festival of Love that there is a great outpouring of energies from the Christed station to all ones upon the planet that they would have opportunity to begin to manifest that which is their perfection or their Christed state. It is a bathing and an outpouring of the Christed energies upon the ones of the planet.

What can you tell us about a being that walked our planet about 400 years ago called Nostradamus, and the accuracy of his predictions?

MONKA   You ask of this one called Nostradamus. And you ask of the accuracy of his predictions. To answer your first question, I shall not be as one that would speak of another, for I have not that right. But with your permission, I shall speak of that which is known to you as prophecy.

Man on planet Earth has been most eager for prophecy. He looks to us, he looks to soothsayers, he looks to all ones to tell him what's going to happen tomorrow. This cannot be done. For tomorrow depends on all that happens today. We make generalized observations. This beloved one also made observations according to what was known at

that time. But recognize with all predictions and all observations, man of Earth has choice. And as he chooses, so goes
his tomorrow. This free will choice is given by divine right,
and intercession cannot be made to remove this choice.

Anytime anyone comes to you -- and this includes
myself -- and we speak of upcoming events, it is said with the
recognition that man of Earth, by his own free will has the
ability to alter what is seen at that hour.

I will add an additional thought. In our dimension, in
all dimensions but your own, there is not time. But we see
things, we see actions, activities as cycles of events. And
one event will follow another event, which will follow another,
and so on to complete a specific cycle within the Divine Plan.
Man of Earth has free will choice as to how long it will take
him to go through the varying stages of events within a cycle.
And so, even though, predictions are given to you and
specific dates are given, specific years upon your calendar,
this is subject to change because of man's free will choice.

I would also share another thought with you. Many
ones that would speak of prophecy and would speak with
great authority, are ones that see visions, or see what they in-
terpret as happenings upon your planet. Recognize that the
weakest link of this is the individual interpretation of what is
seen, for man in his present dimensional state has his own
interpretation in the most limited manner. His state of awareness, his conscious knowingness is at such a level that he is
hampered in making his observation of that which he has
seen or experienced. Those that would speak of your cyclic
events on Earth must do so recognizing that one event follows another. But no specific frame of time reference can be
placed upon these because that is left up to the individuality
that is known as Earth man.

I recognize I have not specifically answered your
question, but I trust I have opened a new door of awareness
for you.

Would you discuss the three days of darkness that have been prophesied?

SARNA ...Throughout your recorded history, various ones have spoken as prophets, and they have prophesied a period that is known as the three days of darkness. These have been described in varying ways. Some have said that the Earth would be swept clean and there would be that which would be a new Earth that would emerge in three days. There are those that have said that there will be the swarm of locusts that will spread across the face of Mother Earth, devouring all. And those that would be of safety would be those that would be indoors, that they would have their windows barred, that they would not see that which is out, for lest, the locusts would enter and devour them also.

There are those that have spoken of storms, of great balls of fire that would dance of the heavens. And each one has, in their own prophecy, given a specific date, a specific time, a specific place. And more importantly, specific instructions have been given that each should follow in minute detail.

I would ask you a question. Have these instructions been ones of love, of assisting, of holding forth the hand to help the neighbor, to help the brother? Have these instructions been ones to share of your individual bounty? Have they been that which has lessened fear and caused ones to stand straighter in their own totality? Have these prophecies been ones of God's anger, of His wrath, of punishment to those that do not believe as another believes? Or have these prophecies been one of love, in which one is lifted to a heightened awareness, to a greater knowing or understanding?

I challenge each upon the planet to remember what they are and who they are. For they are divine essences that have come from Creator Source. They are that which is known as their eternal soul. Why does that which is known as Earth man put such great energy in his physical preserva-

28

tion and so little into that which is his eternalness?

I understand there is a comet that will pass between the sun and the Earth. Will it effect the electromagnetic field of the Earth?

SOLTEC Greetings and salutations. ...The question you have presented is that which concerns the theory of a comet that is coming to your vicinity, and by this I mean your particular portion of the Cosmos.

Are you also aware of that which is coming but has not been defined by many ones upon your planet, that which is now currently, has just left, the Saturnean pattern? This is a -- and here I will hesitate for your scientists are at a loss to describe this that is coming -- I will merely say that there is a composite that is approaching and shall possibly present itself as a moon for you upon your planet.

There are many prophecies, and these that you would speak of as comets; as this I would speak of as the ship that is coming; as you would speak of that which has been given to you by ancient ones; there are many prophecies that are pointed to this particular portion of your cycle, for this is the end of your cycle.

What happens is relative. It is relative to you, the workers of Light, and the balance and stability, the evolvement that comes about. That which is your future is not written within the mighty ledger. And here I must qualify that for it is that it is written within the mighty ledger, but how this comes about is not written, for there are numerous possibilities of happenings for you upon your planet. It is according to you, the workers of Light, and those that are bound to planet Earth, as to what happens.

There is possibility of that which you call the comet. There is possibility of that which is the ship that defies your earthly description. There is possibility that portions of your continents shall be rearranged. There is possibility of great waters. All of these are possibilities. As you would open your hearts in brotherhood, as you would feel a oneness with that which is your earth mother and you would assist her, so it is that many of these possibilities shall not have to manifest.

Oft times, you upon your planet are told of specific happenings that will happen at a certain point on your calendar. And what do you do? You do one of two things. You either put your hands over your ears, bury your head beneath your pillow and forget about the whole thing, or you put great energy into a positive reaction to a foretold event. Hence, it does not happen. Then you would look at that one that has brought forth the truth and you would say, "They aren't very good because it didn't happen that way." In truth, what has happened, you have altered that which would happen...

But as you are aware of the possibility of these events and you concentrate a positive Light in those areas, so it is that you manifest a perfection in that area. Hence, your catastrophe does not happen. So just as you, the ones that are sitting in this room have the potential to do this, so are other ones all over your planet, and this is something that you as the workers of Light, do. And you do this oft times in a state that you are not aware of.

Is it wise at this time to use old Egyptian gods for archetypes?

HATONN In reply to your question, my brother, the answer is no. You of your planet are determined to bring up that which is moldy and archaic, and set it before you as the epitome of all that is. Can you not realize you have all within you to be what you need to be. The shovels that you need to use are those which you can use internally. Recognize there is but one Creative Source. May I repeat myself for clarification. THERE IS ONE CREATIVE SOURCE. You of your planet refer to this source in many ways according to your religious upbringing or according to your studies. When you recognize your attunement with the Creative Source, and you are in at-one-ment state with all of creation, then you will be as you were intended to be, and you will have learned your lessons sufficiently upon your planet.

I ask your indulgence with my emphasis upon this topic, but as we observe many ones upon our monitors in varying places about your planet, we note that there is a great out-cropping of studying, of discussing, of re-implementation that which was found on the old papyrus. Man on Earth is searching. But he is searching externally for that which is within him. Again man is looking to an external source for that which is within him. You must recognize who you are and why you have come. That is your lesson. That is your realization upon your planet. No one of ancient history, no one of your compatriots has that answer for you. It's all within you.

* * * * *

Thank you gentlemen for the thoughts shared. We will close this portion until next we come together. Peace be with you. Remember we come in love. We come in peace. We come in universal brotherhood.

Sarna, out.

THE GOVERNMENTAL SYSTEMS

Greetings in the Light of the Most Radiant One. Sarna here. This portion for discussion concerns the various governmental systems about your planet and their impact upon the peoples of Earth. In the truest sense, to govern is to act as a counselor and teacher to assist others in making their own determinations. Governments are a tool to help those who abide within the government to grow to the utmost of their potential. One selected for a position in governing should reflect only qualities of wisdom, love, experience, and truth.

The originating fathers of the government of the United States carried such concepts as they put forth the basis of the governmental structure. Has it remained the same as their intent? Have those which it governs allowed for the creation of a system which defies limitation or accountability? Who is the server and who is served? These questions and others find answers in the following discussion.

* * * * *

Greetings, brothers and sisters of planet Earth. I am Pahotec. As some of you are aware my primary responsibility with the Fleet is to monitor the governmental systems upon your planet, the one that is known as the Emerauld.

I would ask you to turn your attention for a moment to a view beyond the single governmental system you are familiar with or that you have an awareness of. Planet Earth originally started, if you will, as a one world or a one world planet governmental system. The reason for this was because, one, the population was not large -- it was concentrated in specific areas. And hence there was not the need for the variety and level of government functions which you now enjoy. It is only as you have spread in your population about your planet and you have developed specific isolation attitudes that various individual governments have come into being.

These have been brought into being as a result of a desire and a need for power. And ones have been convinced -- and I speak here of years, many, many years gone by -- ones have been convinced that the only route to survival was to pledge their allegiance, give their support and release their power to that which is called a government.

The original idea of a government was that in which ones governed themselves. Those who were selected as leaders were ones selected because of their wisdom, their understanding and their development. These were ones who were elders who came together and by a voice, a common cry, were selected as the representatives of the peoples of areas.

However, that whole process has changed slightly, upon your planet, shall we say. And your governmental systems have become quite cumbersome. In many instances, and I speak not here of specifics, but in many instances they do not represent the peoples which they govern. And ones who are elected or are appointed to specific offices, find once they have reached these offices that they do not have the responsibility, they do not have the authority to carry out many of the promises they had made as they tried most diligently to be selected for the particular office. Hence the governments have become that which is a system -- which the system governs rather than the individuals.

Each of you is aware of the government which is behind the government. And I shall not go into great detail on this other than knowing that you are aware of this. But your system is encouraged, it is nurtured, by your governments behind your governments. Specific actions are brought into being merely by the stroke of a pen or perhaps a phone call and governments are altered radically. Systems are altered.

Much of these functions are done, not by these great elected officials that you see, but ones that work quietly behind the scenes, who have held posts or positions for a long period of time; or they are also key members or ones who perhaps are not in governmental positions, but rather they are ones who are influential within their country as a whole. And this you are aware of. This you know. And ones in your country you could probably name in a nice list.

But the reason that I would ask to speak with you after this brief background, if you will, is to again impress upon you the importance of standing for what you believe in. The Command has gone to the heads of Governments, we have met with government officials and we have talked with them. This has been done for approximately the last 50 years on your calendar. And unfortunately that which we offer in exchange for the reduction of armaments has not been sufficient to encourage the destruction of the armaments.

So we ask now, we come to you who are the peoples of the planet, we ask you to shake off your coat of lethargy. Listen to what is being asked of you from your local leaders, from those of your country and from those of your planet. Listen to what they are asking of you, and stand for what you know is truth. This is saying that you will not go out and carry banners, that you will not cause disruptions, but you will stand for truth. And when that which are the nuclear armaments etc. are brought to your shores, understand why you do not want them there. Let ones who are in office know how you feel.

When rubbish and waste is being piled and collected in bins and put into your waters or buried beneath the face of your planet, ask why, is there not a better method? Ask that your local legislatures, your councilmen, can they not find a better way to do things? Seek, examine, why are there additives put into your foods, what do they do, why are they there? Become not passive citizens, but active citizens who care, who have a voice who speak with the authority of themselves, who have a concern for their land and for their planet. For it is only as you do this, each of you in that which you call a country, that you can begin to come together in worldwide recognition for a planet.

As of that which was your Christ-Mass last year (1989) the forecast has been for cataclysmic changes by your year 1995. That is not far off. Changes come, the degree of change, the severity if you would desire to use that word, is up to each of you, the citizens of planet Earth. Recognize your responsibility. There is naught that is written in stone as would be said. But rather changes come and they can come in such a manner that they do not have to bring about such a complete alteration.

We have the capability to re-route the meteors, this we can do. By Divine direction, this we can do. We cannot do it without. Divine direction can come if the citizens of planet Earth will begin to stand up and be counted that they are ready to take responsibility for their planet, they are willing to overthrow the government behind the government. For the forces of that which are the nature will balance that register most quickly and easily, if it is your desire, you who are on the planet.

Meanwhile we can but stand and tell you of forecasted events that seem highly probable to come into being. We cannot alter these without Divine direction. You are the ones who bring about this direction...

PAHOTEC (comments at the time of the dissolution of the Soviet Union) ...I have asked to speak at this time so you might be briefed, and perhaps be given thoughts about your current governmental upheavals -- particularly that which is called your Soviet Union -- and those countries who have been under the yoke of the intensive control of that government.

As you will recall, this release or, shall we say, expulsion from the control mechanism known to you as Communism, has become intense. Individuals and countries have catapulted from this form of government to eagerly form governments of their own. This process is no different than any physical process, and indeed, the laws which govern the physical reactions or the physical actions, govern the same in the way of governments. To illustrate: Take a container and fill it with a semi-soft, semi-firm -- whichever word you would choose -- ingredient. Then add a screw press to the top of the container. As the press is turned, indeed, the area of movability is greatly decreased until this semi-firm, or semi-soft component contained is brought to the position it can no longer be contained within the vessel and maintained under the pressure of the press. Hence, the vessel breaks, and the semi-liquid, semi-solid component is then free to ooze about until it defines its own space.

This same process has been going on in this part of your planet. Part of this pressure has been exerted by the Illuminati, and part of this pressure has been exerted by the physical needs of the individuals who make up these various governmental portions or outlines -- that which you would call countries. The belly which gnaws in hunger or shivers in cold revolts at the conditions because it knows that is not its purpose or intent.

This one who is known to you as Gorbachev has within his understanding the model for creating a collective of states working together in a harmonious manner so each individual and each individual state, as well as the collective, which is the union, may prosper. This is not a union or a model for a union which is based upon armaments, but rather, on an exchange of goods for the betterment of each individual. His primary responsibility is to hold the thought for this model and to assist the leaders of the various states to see of their portion and the benefit their states might reap from such a marriage.

The peoples of these countries or states have been in a state of deprivation for so long, they are leaping to the op-

36

posite end of the continuum. Recognize at no extreme points is their growth, but it is only when you have reached the middle ground and you can recognize the attributes and gifts of each extreme, that you might go forth.

Watch well that which is going on in this loosely held together communal marriage, for indeed there are those who are seeking to destroy the model concept held. And many of ones seeking are ones which go far beyond the borders of the represented states, or countries. Remember, those of your governments have two sides to their mouths, and they speak in such a manner which enfuels from both sides.

Watch well that which is going on in your Middle East. Watch well that which is your country which is known as Israel. For indeed, they are playing a scenario they have played before.

The time of isolation and bargaining for positions has indeed run out. Even your country, that which is the U.S. of A., is one in grave political situation. Even as your leaders boast of your prowess -- and in some instances you bully your ways into conferences -- the number of ones within your country who cry from hunger greatly increases. And issues which would truly bring your nation forth as a model for others, are being neglected and relegated to the bottom of the list of priorities.

Watch well your planet, Earth Man. Watch well your planet, my brother and sisters of the stars. Your changes have begun, and even as ones attempt to build from created rubble, so it is, foundations have not been defined. No longer can you be a citizen of your own environs. But it is well that you know what is going on about your planet. Changes are with you. See these, and see them as glorification for a new regime to come forth which might lead peoples in peace...

PAHOTEC (in spring of 1992) ...I have asked to speak with you at this place, this point in your cycle because of the high degree of probability of some unusual events in that which you would call your human community.

Even as you have seen the governments -- or, shall I say, government -- dissolve of the Great Bear into many smaller ones, so it is other countries, other governing bodies shall find they too are in this experience.

Even as I speak of your governments, please note, I too am focusing in on those institutions within your governments which have great impact upon the individual life-streams. You have built such organizations, such institutions, such systems. Indeed, it has been long forgotten who originated these. Rather, it would seem your systems are ruling you.

There has come to our awareness, according to the outcome of the election in your United States, there shall be a great quaking of that which you call your Stock Market. This will happen before the end of this calendar year. If all goes as desired by the "illumined ones," this quaking shall merely be one to bring the small investor into line. However, if the subliminal messages, the ELFs (extra low frequency), and the EHFs (extra high frequency), have not produced the desired effect, then expect a great drop in this market.

The United States is in that which is known as a recessive economy or economic margin. We see plans to maintain this state and it shall spread more globally than ones realize. Those countries who have felt they would not be touched shall find they experience a high degree of impact. Many, many of those things, those institutions which are known as private ones in the U.S. and ones which are partially governmentally subsidized in others, shall be most, most tenuous.

To bring this into language easily understood, your insurance programs shall begin to fold and to crumble -- even those which are partially subsidized by their governments. The whole profession which is seen as the health profession is going to go through an intense period of examination and accountability. Doctors, your healing physicians, shall lose their licenses to practice. Healing facilities which you call hospitals and clinics shall be closed, and the access and availability of treatment for the masses shall be minimized. This is a concerted effort to decrease the population upon the planet.

This is not what I would call a joyful presentation; however, we see ones who are developing healing abilities and techniques. We see ones who shall be miraculously cured because of their belief. We see more and more manifestation to meet individual needs and a general reassessment by individuals as to their priorities and their needs. It has begun. This cannot be emphasized too much. IT HAS BEGUN. Do not be surprised. Do not look for the morrow, but look at the moment and the changes which are being experienced in that moment...

May each of you re-evaluate and re-assess your position for those which are the days before you. We ask you would take the information which we have shared with you into your heart of hearts so you might advise yourself of your necessary steps, your actions...

HATONN Greetings, ladies and gentlemen. ...I would ask of each of you that you might hold all of your leaders in governments in love, in Light, that they might be guided by the Divine Wisdom that is freely shared with them, that they might be receptive to those thoughts, those ideas, those visions that are shared with them for the betterment of those they serve, as well as for universal brotherhood throughout your planet and throughout the total universe.

Why is it that our governments have kept all information concerning space beings from us?

HATONN ...Your government, as well as most governments of Earth, is a state or is in a state of egomania. Each strives to convince its people that they are the superior force within a specific area.

I would ask you for a moment to gaze upon your country and those that lead your country. This is a mighty nation, this nation of your United States of America. It was founded on principles that were divinely brought forth. And these were written by the hand of Masters embodied on your Earth. Great ones volunteered to come forth to serve during your countries inception. And since the day that your country has declared its independence and has stood for the rights of free men, that it has stood for the ideals of brotherhood and of the Great White Brotherhood this has been a country that has been respected. For those of other countries about your Earth that have been put down, that have been down-trodden, they have looked to this country, to ones of this country with admiration and respect. Thus, this has been the state that your country has earned. Now unfortunately, as your country has progressed from its ideal state, the idea of being the greatest, the most perfect and the most powerful has stayed with ones of government.

Now, would you be the greatest and the biggest and the most perfect and the most powerful if you acknowledged there was a force outside this Earth that could communicate with you? A force you have not seen. A force that has vehicles, has ships, that cannot be touched by your bullets, by your warheads. Ones, that when you draw near in a hostile manner, they merely disappear. Would this make you feel superior and comfortable if you acknowledged this to the peoples that you govern?

Unfortunately the approach has been, no. "So we shall be silent upon all of this. We shall not acknowledge a presence external to Earth. We shall acknowledge no superior force except our own." Though I assure you, ones in high government offices have heard from us directly. And there has been a very specific communication with your country and with other predetermined countries within your world.

What do you see as being the response to information about interstellar contact if the government would release this?

SARNA ...It would bring about mass hysteria for most of the collective. It would bring about a mass hysteria. Man on planet Earth does not like to accept anything but the fact he is the superior, and he does not recognize he has not all the answers. And in some ways he is a child in the growth process. But he is a child for reason. And because there are ones about the Cosmos who are as represented on your planet in all varying levels of evolution and growth, the Cosmos -- the ones representing life within the Cosmos -- represent just as large a continuum. And so you have many ones out there, and you have many ones who have had a variety of experiences. And unfortunately, your media does not sell well when it is something good that happens. It only sells well when it is something that is a phenomena or it is frightening, hmm?

Look at what goes on on your planet itself. When you would watch that which is the news, does it tell you of the wondrous things which are done from one neighbor to another? No, it does not say this. But it tells you who was robbed; it tells you who was hurt. For that seems to be the desired impact, hmm?

MONKA (at the time of the Los Angeles riots) Blessings in the Light of the most Radiant One. ...I would select to speak to you at this hour of that which you would call your current events. What is happening on your planet? Some of you immediately would say to me, "We have problems." Man is taking his brother's life, and man is setting fire to his buildings, is he not? You have been told about these things. Now what are their blessings? For recognize, there is no thing which happens which does not have a blessing in it.

In this place which you would call your "place of angels" (Los Angeles) there has been great unrest, has there not? What is its blessing? ("Brings people together.") It brings people together. ("Fires cleanse.") The fires cleanse. ("An opportunity to balance.") An opportunity to balance. ("There are some people who did some bad things and stole some things who have come to the realization that it was wrong, and they took them back. And so, they had an awakening, a realization.") What else? ("It brings to the attention of all of us that there are many throughout the Earth that live in poverty and we need to assist them before they lose their ability to function.")

I'm going to take your thought for a moment. Is it poverty -- and poverty, the picture that I see is the type of housing and the amount of monies -- this is what Earth man consciousness would say is poverty. But could poverty be that which is the act of removing dignity? And has all of this in the City of Angels been an opportunity for man all over the planet to evaluate what he holds as important; what he holds as qualities of individualism, regardless of that which you call the race or the creed, or any thing which you would set up barriers about? But rather, is this a question in which ones are saying, "I am your brother; please see my dignity as that which is a divine creation"?

So perhaps, could that be what this is? Could it be a cry of the deity within to be recognized as that?

And as you put forth your thoughts during that which was a period of turmoil, what thought did you put forth? What did you learn from the experience -- you as individuals? What did you learn? ("We still tend to put an unbalanced thought into the unbalance, rather than sending forth a balanced thought to assist them.") Did you do that?

When you would see this on your televisions, what kind of thought did you put out? Did you hold it in perfection? Or did you sit there and did you look, and you said, "Isn't that terrible?" You do not have to answer me out loud. Answer within yourself. In a situation such as happened, such as was given the opportunity to be in your City of Angels, do you realize that the focused thought of perfection by one hundred peoples could have stopped it? No, I'm not saying that you would make a judgment in that, you would merely hold the focused thought of the balance and the perfection -- one hundred people. And it couldn't -- it couldn't; it would have been as if walls had come up. You could have watched your television and you could have seen fires go out. Now isn't that a wondrous gift? When are you going to begin to use it?

But what did you do, the collective consciousness which is Earth man about the planet? For the fires, the beatings, the unbalance, were seen in all parts of your planet, when in truth, was it not a cry of man to be seen as an individual who has the dignity of being divine?

It was a wondrous gift, this experience in your place of angels, for ones came together and they assisted. No, these were not ones who you would know about from your distance; but these were ones who quietly helped their brother. There were many Light ones who were involved in the whole process. And though, if you walked up to them and you said, "Are you a worker of the Light?" they would say, "No, the fire was just put out." They wouldn't know what you were talking about at all. They would only know there was a caring for their brother.

See the experiences as blessings, and do not accept the unbalance which an experience brings. For as you do that, what do you do? You add to the unbalance. We held the experience in perfection. There were ones who chose to come aboard the ships during this whole experience. They were brought up, and some would seem that they were rather beaten by the experience, but they have recovered quite nicely. And there were others who had opportunity to come, and they selected to stay because they felt there was work which they needed to do.

There shall be, in your future, for it is lodged well upon your horizon, other instances. And there will be challenges for each of you to see if you can be aware of these and hold the concept of the perfection as your media ones would tell you how terrible it is. Can you hold the concept of the perfection?

There is that which is known to you as the Christ Station, and those within that station see only that which is in the perfection which is within each of you, which is within all situations. And so, they bring harmony to disharmony. They bring joy to that which has brought a tear...

Does it not take a catastrophe or catastrophes to awaken people, to bring us to our senses so we are aware of what we are here for?

MONKA ...Indeed it seems to be that you must have some great unbalance for ones to awaken to themselves and to what they are capable of doing. But if all ones would see of the perfection in any situation, it does not mean the situation necessarily will be totally altered, but it does mean that it will carry a different impact...

I said to you earlier, if one hundred people had focused on the perfection, they could have altered what happened in your place of Angels (riots in Los Angeles). Please note that which is my wording: They "could have." I did not say that they would have. And the reason I say that is because when ones come together to focus their thought, their energies on any thing which is beyond themselves, they must always do this according to Divine Will, for there is a plan beyond which you know and there are many intricate details with which you are not familiar. And so, to focus, to share, to be an instrument for Divine Energy, ask always you do this according to Divine Will. And then there may be a point at which you would come away and you would say, "We were ineffective." But perhaps there was a lesson there which was greater than you could recognize. But you have done your part, because you have aligned with the Divine Will...

You have discussed the United States, but could you tell us about the role of Australia?

KEILTA Greetings, dear ones of planet Earth. ...This area of land of which you speak upon your planet, if you can visualize it is sleeping. It has not awakened to its role. And the ones who have inhabited this area have not awakened to their role either. It is anticipated at this place in your cycle, which might change, there shall be great earth changes in the area, but the autonomy of the land will be maintained. There will be shifts and changes there but the land itself will be maintained.

When there has been an unbalance in other places within your planet there are ones within your area who will step forward as leaders, as counselors. No they are not recognized at this moment. They do not recognize themselves. The government shall take a rapid shift from your existing one. Do you know that which is the term caretaker government, have you heard of this? ("Yes.") This is what you are in. For there are ones who will come forth who will be great shining beings to offer counsel and assistance to the rest of the planet. However, there must be the wait until that time.

You will find on your particular, shall we call it a large island, that there will be a great interest, intensity of interest in that which would be called new age material, particularly that which has to do with the brethren of the stars. You will find also there will begin to be a great interest in that which are the technical books, thoughts which have been shared by ones of the stars. There will be awakened a hunger within ones as they begin to feel the energies and to grow with the energies and to feel the expansion...

MONKA (adds) ...You have a variety of levels of consciousness within your country, do you not? And each particular group coming together within your country represents a particular consciousness. Some of these, you are aware, are not compatible, hmm? So your country has the potential of coming apart as an iceberg would because of the diversity of energies of ones within your country.

Your country, or that which you see as your country, as you are aware, is a portion of that which was Atlantis. It was a linking area between Atlantis and Lemuria. And you are aware of this, huh? At that point within your own cycle of experience, the consciousness which pervaded this land mass was a melding of consciousness of the aspects of your own development. That which is your country was a high plain area. And as they would feel physical changes, the high plains area became ocean frontage.

Now, and at that point, you, by your consciousness, elected to retain this plateau area. Because of the diversity of the ones who have incarnated in this area, there is now that which is the opportunity for breaking apart, or separating, and there will be portions which will have opportunity to sleep a little while, and there will be those which will become much more mountainous, shall we say, or have a higher altitude.

The collective consciousness -- and here I speak not of the workers of the Light, I speak of the general populace, please understand this -- the consciousness within your area is one which is content. Most ones are not looking beyond their immediate physical needs. What can you do about this, is your next question, right? As you come together with ones of like kind, you intensify your own actions. For example, if there are five of you who come together to hold a specific thought, a specific concept for a period of time, it is likened to fifty of you. So each one of you can, in your circle, you can multiply by ten. For that is the energy which you bring forth and the energy which is shared with you to intensify the energy which might be shared.

May I suggest to you, you actively come together. And groups who have felt an isolation to look for others about whose philosophy is likened to your own, that you might share in the intensification of the energy which comes through you for your portion of your country.

During this period it is most vital, if that would be appropriate word, to help to stimulate others in your region to begin to look beyond their immediate gratification. Can you do this? May I suggest that you would come together in groups, hold your area in Light -- and this has been said so many times of so many specific areas, it is an overused and abused thought, to hold something in Light, for we hear this said by many ones upon your plane, and truly I feel oft times you do not understand what this means -- but if you would come together in a circle or in a group and you would allow the energy to flow through you for all ones in your region for their highest good.

Do not try to concentrate a specific Light here, there, or say that you want ones to awaken. Visualize your region as you are looking at it from above, and see it truly in a golden mist which permeates every inch of your land, and every drop, every cell of each one's being. Make this commitment as group, as twosomes, as threesomes, or however many of you who come together. And then, be alert to what is going on within your region, for you may see and experience change within the collective consciousness of the populace...

And New Zealand?

DIONUS Salutations, Eartheans. ...You are going to be entering a war. And it is not a war of weapons but it is a philosophical war. For there will be ones who will come forth and they will try, shall we say, to encourage your population to enter into a system in which you lose your sovereignty. How do you like that? And it is only by being able to maintain your vibration and to speak your truth that you can keep your mountain tops above the waters.

When I speak these words or share these thoughts I do not place this responsibility solely upon your shoulders, but I place this trust upon the shoulders of all ones of Light who desire peace and harmony upon their planet.

You who have not been as vocal in the monetary system of your planet, shall find you have opportunity to become more vocal. Sovereignty. Soul Reign. Soul-reignty. For the past four, five decades upon your planet, Workers of the Light have been relatively quiet, ones who whispered there association with others, hmm? You are now in a position that you take what you know to be truth and you live it, so all might see. No this does not mean that you carry a banner which says, "I am Working Light". But it is that you stand for truth and for principle. This is in the market place, this is in your government, this is in dealing with your neighbors and with your family.

Of a distant day most of you were quiet when you saw changes coming and you took sacred teachings and technologies and you hid them well that they would not be abused or misused. I speak to you this hour to say to you, your trial of silence is coming to a close. Your trial or your trust of standing in your own Light, knowing others walk beside you, is with you...

New Zealand has declared itself nuclear free. Could our government be persuaded by the United States to again allow nuclear ships to dock here?

DIONUS ...And why could he be persuaded? ("Well, national governments have always been frightened of America") Let it be known by your voice and your actions that this will not be tolerated by the peoples of your country, so there is no question within your leaders minds as to what the peoples would desire.

Ones can be persuaded because pressure can be put upon them, not by the governments so much, as by the governments behind the governments, and who is controlling who, where?...

48

You did not come to your island, to your country to sit by and to watch your valleys go under waters. Long have you stayed on the mountain tops and the valleys have grown fertile as they have rested beneath the waters. Give them opportunity to come up that you might reap the harvest.

I was in China until just before the disaster happened in Tiananmen Square in 1989 and it didn't feel like it was going to go that way. It felt like such a time of hope. I'm wondering if what did happen there was supposed to happen that way or if it could have been different?

SARNA ...It could have been different. The intent and the infusion and the desire was that there would be a peaceful marriage between that which was the old and that which is the new -- that there would be a coming together and there would be a sharing, recognizing that neither had an absolute understanding. But by coming together and sharing, the wisdom of the old could meld with the ideology and the enthusiasm of the new.

However, shall we say there were some strings that were pulled. I believe you call it "buttons pushed" or "chains rattled" or some such thing, and ones were reminded that this could not be allowed to go forth. However, the voice has not been stilled. It is a whisper and it continues and it will continue because this was an example for Earth mankind of a peaceful marriage -- of a coming together of ideologies and the respect for that which had been done, and the enthusiasm of that which could be done. And this was the intent.

There were ones that took on embodiments specifically from the Fleet to be involved in this process, to assist in this process, and it was our sorrow. And there were many ones, though it will not be easily recognized at this point, but there were ones that their soul energies were removed from the forms that the perfection that they were trying to bring

49

forth would be infused in another form or another body at another time. So there was not the massacre, shall we say, because we were closely monitoring what was going on and when these ones, when it appeared that there would be damage that would be of a great wounding to their souls, they were quickly removed from the forms.

It felt to me as though part of it was triggered by all of the negative projections from the rest of the world on what was going to happen -- the fear that that would happen. Did that have anything to do with it?

SARNA This had impact but the true triggering was by that which would be called your "government behind your government", the government of your world that is behind the governments of your world. This was the true triggering. What you experienced was the negative flow that was coming. However, there were many ones about the planet that were sending forth great thoughts of love and balance and respect for the attempt, for the accomplishment of what was to come into being.

However, to have let this come into being would have been an acknowledgement of a philosophy that was one of not control and was a philosophy of individuals coming into their own power and claiming their own rights and standing ready to be accountable for what they claimed. And this could not be tolerated, for if it had been tolerated there could have been a mass revolt about the planet. And that could not be allowed by your government behind your governments.

What is likely to happen in China in the future?

PAHOTEC ...This country shall we say is a sleeping lion that trembles in its sleep... These ones, the leaders of this particular country, look around and they see how other leaders are altering their style of government in order that there might be more participation. They also note that ones are not prepared to participate. Their desire is to keep things as a status quo. However, they recognize this cannot be done. For indeed there are too many who have embodied within this portion of your planet who have great strength within them. So it a case of sitting and waiting. The lion sleeps but it knows that the hunter is quite close. It merely rests with one eye open. And there is little regard or discussion with the other countries of your planet for it has been observed there is great wisdom in maintaining one's silence and autonomy.

Could you tell us more about the breaking up of the Soviet Union?

DIONUS (at the time of the dissolution of this country) ...The Eastern Bloc countries and that which has been your rival for a long period of time, that which you would call Russia, there has been great strife in this area. Ones easily picked on the vibration to revolt. This one that is known as the leader (Gorbachev) in your country that is known as Russia is one that has worked most closely with guidance and went into a situation in which the odds were very great against him accomplishing what he was capable of doing, for his desire was to free people. And his desire was to see economies and countries in which countries could stand in their autonomy and not be swept up by a one this or a one that.

Unfortunately that which he inherited was archaic. All of the monies of this country, of this union had gone toward the making of armaments and putting on a show that the rest of your world would know they were superior in this area. As these ones had their freedom it went more quickly than it was desired for it to happen because he had instruction, guidance, if you will, that he could help each one of these countries to be part of the union that makes up the Russian union but the country would not declare and be autonomous until they had the capacity to be autonomous.

51

So what has happened? There were a few little vibrations that went in there and had everyone stirred up very quickly, hence you had mass revolts that came about very quickly. Ones were revolting against they didn't know what, they were just revolting against and they had no thought of what they were going to be for. And this is evidenced now. And even as you will notice in your media there is no discussion of what is going on in this part of your planet. Peoples are disillusioned, peoples are hungry. There is not the production because the factories are not capable of this. So there is great unbalance in this particular portion of your planet.

That country which is known to you as Russia, there is great unbalance. Because if you take steps as they are to be taken, one after the other, you can reach your objective in an organized manner in which there is benefit for all ones. You add an extra zap of wave here and there and you speed it up so there is no order to this. There is merely that which is a milling around and an unbalance and an uncertainty.

That which is known to you as Russia has put much of its gold on the market in an effort to try to have a way to stimulate the economy within the country so that peoples might be fed. Peoples are disillusioned because they have not had the opportunity to go through the steps to reach their goal. They have been placed from point 'A' to point 'D' with nothing in between.

This is a critical situation upon your planet for ones who are leaders, ones who have great guidance, ones who truly are workers of Light, are working Light, are feeling very threatened. They cannot work with the population of their countries because the masses or the populations of their countries do not know what they want. Right now that portion of your planet is being manipulated and controlled by ELF. It has been the desire that the world population not be aware of this until that particular block of countries is well in control. When it is in control you have that one particular block which will be one economy, one monies...

Gorbachev is a walk-in, is this correct?

DIONUS ...There are some who would call a walk-in that which is a consciousness of one who has expanded to a greater consciousness of that which they already carry. And perhaps you might consider this as the walk-in in this particular instance... As far as our patterns show he has had some experiences that have been quite enlightening for him and expanding. He came in with the knowledge that he would have to expand and in this process he would have to take on karma for his country and this is what in some instances he is doing. And he is trying to assist his country to rise above the karmic pattern.

Is it true that the Russians have a large space station orbiting Earth now?

HATONN ...Yes, there is an "island" above Earth that is circling it, and it was placed there by the country that is known as the U.S.S.R. And there is sophisticated equipment on smaller satellites that have been placed, that circle your Earth that have been placed there by your country that also is monitoring all that is transpiring. So in truth you are spying on those who are spying on you. And you have quite a vicious circle going.

What about the Middle East?

MONKA ...As you of Light are aware we have expended great energies in the area of your world that is known as your Middle East. Ones in this area are replaying a scenario that was once played at the time of Atlantis. These ones strive for the elusive recognition of their peers. They strive they think for that which they call freedom. Yes they are striving for freedom, but it is not that state that is known as an earthly one. The true freedom that they are seeking is that in which their soul comes forth to speak in equality with their being.

This divine portion has been locked so tightly within for these many eons that it is fighting a last battle to come forth to be in balance with the new coming energies. It is that this divine portion asks to be heard, to be known, to be at one with the rest of the being.

This is the struggle that they are feeling. However they are interpreting these stirrings as ones for recognition of the physical being, of the securing of a space of land, that they might call forth the honor of their homelands. In truth there is no homeland, but their is the state of being at home in this vehicle of embodiment. There is the answer. But as with many things that are being experienced at this hour, the interpretation of that which is felt, and that which is done as a result of the feeling, is quite different. Man is quite determined to close off his ear to his inner guidance...

There is a great energy source in the area of the Middle East that is being used by the dark brothers to cause unbalance and confusion. At the present this has been encapsulated, and those ones that are tempted by its energies are covered to allow those ones of us to regroup and seek guidance to alleviate this critical condition.

Here might I also add, that as you share of love and Light with ones in this area that you share it in a specific manner. The reason for this is that as you send it forth in a shotgun manner that it causes a measure of unsettling and confusion as it is received by ones there. If the love and Light is sent forth specifically, such as for ones to feel of peace and balance or to be at one with the creative process, then that is how the energy goes forth. It does not cause the unsettling or the measure of the confusion that is the result of sending forth love and Light. There is great love energies in this area, there is great Light that is shared with all ones of this portion of your globe. This can cause some of the confusion that is felt for the ones in the recipient position are feeling confusion and unbalance at all that is coming to them. I merely offer this for your consideration.

KEEOTA (in spring of 1992) Greetings in the Light of the Infinite Source. ...You are aware of all the struggles which have been going on in that which you call your Mideast, in that country which is known as Iraq. May I add to your understanding a little at this time...

There has been a door which has been closed, a door or a portal which has been closed which cuts off a vibration of a specific frequency. Shall we say, for your understanding, it is a vibration which is cut off from coming to man. It is one of the denser vibrations. This door began to be closed approximately five years on your calendar. And here I would say, when I give you such dates or such times, recognize I am not completely tuned with your time frames. But to the best of my understanding, this would be about when this has happened. This door began to be closed, and what it has done is, there are ones on your planet who have operated in this vibration for a long period of time, and it has been quite unsettling to them. And so, they have reacted to this. And by closing this portal to the more densely-tuned vibrations, it has allowed a more fine attunement throughout the planet.

Now ones who have been accustomed to a more dense vibration are finding they are quite uncomfortable at this point with the more fine attunement. Hence, they have a great unbalance. You will notice that, as this door was closing, that on your last calendar year you had a war in that which is called your Middle East, and countries came together as allies who have not operated as allies before and have no great desire to do so in the future. But because of the circumstances, they were brought together, primarily out of fear. They, too, have reacted and are reacting to the more finely-tuned vibrations which are about your planet.

Now this one that you call Iraq -- and perhaps I will give you a, shall we say, four-dimensional geography lesson here -- this country that you call Iraq is most unique. It might be looked upon as the cradle of spiritualism for your planet. And I will leave that thought; I will not pursue it any further...

But note, over this area there is a large etheric portal. This is where your ley lines which you see in a three-dimensional way are also going up and through your earth, completely through your earth, along your earth's surface, above the surface of your earth, and coming at various angles. There is a portal through which we may enter and leave with a minimum of disturbance in this area which is called Iraq when -- and may I underscore tenfold the word "when" -- there is balance within that area. You will note for a great many, many, many, many years on your planet there has been no balance in that area -- so our responsibility, our job, has been to maintain this portal, this etheric portal, regardless of what is going on within the ley lines, which is being experienced within the ley lines upon your planet. You can now understand the need for the number of ships, the amount of involvement, and the reason for this.

There are other portals about your planet -- etheric portals about your planet. But this one appears to have the most difficulty in its maintenance, shall we say, because of the evolutionary level of the ones on the planet in this vicinity.

There is also a large portal, if you will, over that which would be called your eastern European countries. Even as we can travel in and out of this portal to come into your dimension or out of it quite easily, there must be maintenance to maintain it, for it is a coming together of ley lines. As there is the disruption of vibration by warring, by disagreement, by unbalance of any sort within a 1,000-mile radius of the portal, then it is, the whole vibration of the portal is altered, making it more difficult for our entrance or our exit.

It has been because of the evolutionary level of most of the ones in this area which is called your Middle East, much energy has been concentrated to maintain a stability of the portal. The Third Galaxy has been particularly involved in this, shall we say. My beloved Keilta has been quite involved in this. Indeed, there have been instances that he and his ship have become quite battered as he would be within the portal, trying to maintain its vibration, and there would be a sudden impact of unbalance which would cause a squeezing as if to close the portal. It has not been an easy assignment for those who have had that assignment...

You will note as the final stages of this portal is closing how much of your governments topsy-turvy has come about, hmm? -- such as your banking system and other things involving your legislators...

We nearly always seem to have warring factions in the Middle East. Will the Space Command allow nuclear warheads to meet each other in the skies in these or any other wars on this planet?

DIONUS ...One, before they would come together they would be neutralized. So, if you would have that which would coming together, you would not have the problem that would be seen to be created.

What you have, and I presume you are asking this because of this Middle Eastern situation upon your planet -- have you observed small boys and one draws a line in the sand and he says, "If you step over here, my brother will beat you brother." And another one, as they get a little older, they draw the line and they say, "If you step over there, I'll beat you up." And then the boys get a little older and they say, "My army will beat your army."

This which is being played, was played at a time in Atlantis. The same ones are involved in this scenario. This one whom you look at as the bad guy (Saddam Hussein), desperately wants out of the situation he has placed in. But, because of his makeup, his own understanding, he does not know how to do this.

From our observations of his pattern he was in great debt to that which you would call the Illuminati as well as to other countries. And what better way to get out of debt to a country than to take it over, uh?...

Could you talk to us about the hostage taking that goes on in the Middle East and the terrorists who are doing it?

MONKA (given at the time of the hostage crisis) ...Though these ones that you call hostages are in areas that are unfamiliar to them at this time there is a great lesson here for each of them. And they are being given the opportunity to learn their lesson. There are ones that had lost their way, that had indeed taken of many side trips to their path. These ones have had opportunity to recognize of their brief sojourns, and to offer their commitment and their vow to come forth into the Light. Still other ones whose faith has shown as the brightest Light has grown even stronger. And their Light and their intensity has grown, for their faith has not wavered and they have been secure in their love for their Divine Creator. These ones that you know as the hostages are watched over by ones of the Angelic Realms. They are ministered to by ones that are unseen by mortal eye.

I would ask you each for one moment to think of these ones that are holding the captives. In your minds eye these are terrorists. These ones are committing a most unpardonable act, am I not correct? I know it is so. But in truth these ones -- and I speak of those that are not the leaders but those that follow a philosophy -- these are ones that are crying for help, that are crying for love, that are crying for an opportunity for individual identity in an area that is an area of mass identity and mass hysteria. These ones feel they have sons, they have fathers, they have husbands that have been taken and held as hostages in another place. In their frustration, in their lack of identity, they have seized this opportunity to be recognized, and to have their voice heard.

Their intent, as observed by us, has not been one of harm. Their intent has been one of a cry, yea, a plea for assistance and for recognition. Each of you that sit within this circle this night have your own identity. You know, you feel of your purpose. You have reached a measure of attunement with your Creator, and you partake most freely of the gifts from above that are shared with you. Your existence on your present plane is not one of deprivation. Indeed, you have food that fills your bellies. You have clothing that protects you from the elements. You have homes that keep you safe from the elements.

These ones that you call terrorists do not have these luxuries. Many of them have lost their homes. They have been herded from one place to another. They have not had sufficient foods to fill their bellies, and their families, their family members have been scattered. Do you wonder at their cry? Would you too not cry as they cry? They ask to be seen, to be recognized, as individuals, as HU-men. They seek not to harm, that is not their intent. They seek to have family members restored to families. They seek to have family units united. They seek for land on which they might grow foodstuffs to fill themselves. They seek the opportunity to build shelters that they might be protected from the elements. It is not their intent to harm these ones that they have taken to bargain their plea. This is not their intent. But should the worldly pressures become sufficient, and should ones in positions of leadership yield to the persuasion of those of the lower brotherhood, then there shall be blood upon the land. And there shall be weeping upon the heart. But this shall not be if we of the Fleet and you ones of Light on Mother Earth hold these ones in love, hold these ones in Light and pray for universal peace...

The topic of one world government and one monetary system brings up fear in many people. We know this is going to come about in time, so how do we help people understand the real reason for one world government, etc.?

JOKHYM Greetings in the Light of the Radiant One. ...First you would speak of one world government. And the individual governments on your planet would quake at this prospect. But what is the purpose of that which is your

United Nations? Is this not to bring about a compatibility of the governing process within the planetary system? Is it not the purpose of this, your United Nations? Does not united nations mean all nations coming together in oneness?

That which we would desire to impart is that the governmental structures would be led by the Divine Force. This would be their guidance, their instruction, and there would be the commonality of love and caring. And the leaders of the various countries would come together in council, such as that which is called your United Nations, that they might consider ways of uplifting man kind, ways of educating, providing foodstuffs, building libraries where man might go and study and learn; where leaders, or potential leaders, might come that they would be honed and polished in the various attributes of government. To govern is to lead, to teach, to care, to share.

Ones cannot be governed if they do not allow this to happen. This is something that is greatly neglected upon your planet. For these ones that would call themselves dictators, that would choose to browbeat, impoverish and misuse their fellow man, are being allowed this by the ones that they are governing. Because there is not education, because there is not understanding, because there is not knowledge, there is not the wisdom, the expertise within the masses to call for ones that would lead, that would govern in a Christ-like manner.

The intent of this which would be called your New Day is to bring this awareness to all ones. And those that would see the entry into governmental positions as one of superiority and domination would quickly find that they do not fit and they would choose to withdraw from the position, for their energies would not be harmonious.

Your greatest leaders are ones that share truth. Your greatest leaders are those that uplift and help to guide all of mankind. This which is your country in America was founded on these basic principles; however, through the misinterpretation and the limitation imposed by man, these basic truths have been greatly modified. Indeed, they have had parameters placed about them that are quite cumbersome. There is but one governing force and that is the Divine Creator. Anything else is but a poor excuse and it will not stand. This is the reason many of your governments now are feeling quite shaky and insecure because they have been based or they have used as their foundation, untruths. And they have not sought to uplift the mankind that has been placed within their trust.

One government is one governing philosophy. This is the primary objective -- to enable each man upon Earth to come into his fullest and his highest potential in any one specific embodiment. For it is as man can come into this awareness, so it will be that the Christed ones will be able to walk among you.

Now, the next question that you have asked is one of the monetary system. The anxiety level that comes up at the thought of one monetary system is phenomenal upon you planet. Your monetary system has been governed by a small, elect group of individuals that indeed play governments and peoples as pawns on a chessboard. You have had a controlled monetary system for well over 150 years but you have not chosen to be aware of this.

The monetary system, this oneness, this one monetary system, would be a system that would be based upon the law of supply and demand -- that which you need, in other words. As there are geophysical changes upon the planet, there shall come into awareness that perhaps the precious stones you wear about your neck do not have the great significance that they once had. Indeed, the loaf of bread will take on a greater significance. So thus would be a situation of barter. It would begin in a rudimentary state such as your loaf of bread for a handful of beans. But it too would grow until there would be a balanced system with no ones controlling the monetary system. But indeed, it would be controlled by the mass of mankind. It would be much more equitable and wealth would be much more easily distributed. For indeed, in this particular era that we are speaking of, there shall be no need to hoard great sums of monies. For indeed, they shall be of no significance. And ones upon the planet will recognize this, and indeed, there shall be an air of cooperation and sharing.

The response that immediately comes forth is that this would be a totalitarian state. And indeed, it would not be. For all men, as your Constitution says, are created equal. This equality, or this translated, means each man has the ability to recognize his highest capability and potential within his state of perfection that he chooses to do. In the New Day this shall be the goal and the objective of each one that is here.

You have been in a state of corruption and as the various changes come about your planet, you shall see this state crumble. Many of you shall feel a limbo as you watch the dissolvement of one way of life to begin another. Many lessons you have received concerning staying centered within the Light. Stay centered in that which you are. This shall be of great value to you as there are abrupt changes upon your planet.

The monetary system shall be one in which there is a greater and more equitable distribution than that which you are experiencing now...

Could you tell us more about the world economy?

MONKA ...Your world economy, it is a sticky wicket is it not? You are in a very precarious state, much more so than you realize. The whole economy that you know and observe is indeed a false one, and of course most of you are aware of that. Those which are called your banking systems, you shall find that more and more of these shall close within your next eighteen month period (through 1991). That isn't long my friends, is it?

As this happens, so far they have been covered by your governments. With an increase in the number of banks that will close this will be more and more difficult. Hence your government will borrow more money. Taxes will go up. Interest rates will go up, and your government behind the government will be smiling for indeed things are going according to plan they feel.

Those of you who would have funds to invest, look seriously at how you would invest these. Though we would have no desire to act as investment brokers to you, we would say to you invest in that which has a return for you such as food, land, and that which you might barter with.

The economy of your planet is as precarious as the economy of your country. Indeed there is no separation in the various economies. As you would look at those which are the new countries in your Eastern Bloc countries, more and more you will see they have no basis to claim. They have no basis for their claim of freedom in the monetary world. Many of these ones have been ones who have merely been used as pawns to bring about change, to bring about an unbalance, to bring about a change in your world monetary system and your economy. These ones find that they will not be able to support the peoples whom they represent. Hence they too shall enter into the borrowing game, further placing themselves in the control of the Illuminati.

At this point, as long as the leaders of your governments play their roles, your stock market and your economy shall continue on as it is for a period, and I will place no date upon this. But it shall depend on what your Eastern Bloc countries are doing, what is going on in your country that is known as Russia, and how much you are willing to be taxed to support and contribute to others about your planet.

Look carefully at your investments. May I suggest to you that you do not place yourselves in great debt recognizing you desire to maintain your sovereignty.

We are watching the whole process most closely and

we will alert you if there are any immediate changes coming about for we have no desire for you who are upon the planet to suffer. However, we have no desire for you to become greedy, either...

Is the social security number going to be our sole identification for commerce, monies etc.? Will it be stamped upon us permanently?

HATONN ...By Divine Decree from the Father-Mother God each of you ones of Earth have been given choice. And no one, I repeat, no one has the ability, has the right to go contrary to Divine Decree. Your choice is your own and that which you do with your choice is your own. Should each of you be content to be branded as cattle, and this is your choice, then so be it.

This is not a new concept, and this is one that has been tossed about in your hallowed halls of government on several occasions. Each time that it is discussed it becomes more and more of an actuality; however, we have been given permission to modify some of the thoughts that are received by particular ones within some of your government agencies.

As you also are aware there are many of us -- and here I speak of the ones of the distant stars, planets, galaxies -- that walk with your leaders of your governments that are involved and attempt to help sway opinions and conclusions that only those thoughts and those concepts of Light shall remain with Earth.

I realize my answer has not been a specific one but in all matters that involve man of Earth's free choice it is most difficult for us to be specific.

* * * * *

Your world is changing. Its wealth is unequal in its distribution. Myopic views cloud the vision. You who are the working Light, carry the trust to open the eye and expand the vision so that all might have opportunity to see with clarity the truth of purpose of planet Earth.

Sarna, out.

THE GOVERNMENTS, ILLUMINATI AND ETs

Greetings in universal brotherhood. I am Sarna to once again coordinate the discussions and questions presented. The topic is one which is of great interest to you on planet Earth. Our participants for this portion are Commanders Ashtar, Jokhym, Keilta, Beatrix, Keeota, Emartus and I. We begin with Commander Ashtar.

* * * * *

In the Light of the Radiant One, I greet you. I am that one who is known as Ashtar... Each of you is aware of that which you call UFO activity about your planet, are you not? And you consider us to be that which is separate from UFO activity. May I suggest to you that you would consider that which is within your dimension and that which is beyond your dimension. Most of the UFO activity you are aware of is that which are of beings traveling within the star systems who are of a similar vibratory pattern to your own. These ones have come from various star systems for various reasons, some of them quite benign and others, not quite so.

Those of the Ashtar Command operate in a multi-dimensional sphere. We can, we have, and we shall, alter the vibrational frequency of our ships so they might be observed by you upon your dimension. Routinely, ordinarily we do not do this. You would ask me, "When will you do it, Commander?" And I will say, "When you are ready for us to do this." When your vibrational pattern is such that you may maintain a compatibility with us, then we can come into your sphere and we can maintain with you for longer periods.

At this point, our entrance into your dimensional vibration is on brief excursions. Most of the encounters you have had with us have been in that which has been a telepathic communique, or in such instances as you have been given a holograph in order that you might have confirmation or verification.

You are aware of the alteration in vibrational field about your planet and the acceleration in your own attunement processes. This is being heightened in order for our vibrational patterns to come into a closer harmony so you might be able to have conscious physical experiences with us. However, at this point, as the physical being is observed and monitored on planet Earth, the number of you who are ready to enter into a physical encounter with that which are the multidimensional ones of the Ashtar Command, are relatively limited.

I merely speak this that you will understand why we do not come in and appear for you when you have put out this desire. There are many ones of you who have, by holographic and telepathic means, been able to see our ships or to have conscious recognition of the experiences you have had when you have been upon the ships. As your vibration is more finely tuned, you will have more of these experiences.

You would say to me, "Commander always promises of what is coming, but why is it not happening now?" I say to you, look at yourselves. Look at how much you have grown. Look at how you have changed, how you have expanded, and yet, you have grown in your ability to focus since first you entered into this path. Do you see what progress you have made? There is still a little more that needs to be made, but I assure you you are coming along in quite an accelerated manner... Many of you have been growing from a mental reference. Your next process is one of an integration of the mental and the heart aspect...

But to continue. We operate within your realms all the time, but the vibrational pattern of our ships is so it is not easily observable by you. As the infusion progresses for planet Earth, more and more of our vessels are within the ethers about your planet. When your eye is ready, you will see it. When your understanding is ready, you will receive the thought. So I ask you, Legions of Light, to continue on your path, to make conscious effort in your integrative processes, for indeed, you are greatly needed at this hour.

I have spoken and I have said that approximately one-third of those who had volunteered in their assignment upon the planet are all that are left, or who have donned their working clothes, shall we say. Two-thirds of the original volunteers have selected to pursue other avenues. Your load, we recognize, is a heavy one. Indeed, most of you are doing double duty, if not triple in some instances. Assignments have had to be shifted. Expanded roles have been willingly assumed by you in order to work with planet Earth and her inhabitants. For this, we salute you.

Before you have reached the, what you would call the cataclysmic part of your Earth changes, you will have ample opportunity to observe us.

Currently there are many ones about your planet who come from a vibrational pattern similar to your own. These ones do not have the integration abilities you have, for indeed, they have come from specialized areas of intellect and mental capacities. Their ships are observable in your skies. I would but caution you, just because you see a ship it does not always mean it is one you would desire to enter. Just as you would question when a vehicle would stop and assist you in your journey down a road, so it is, I would also ask if one invites you to get into their ships, perhaps you might find out what family they represent, where are they from, and a little more about them before you would hop into the vehicle, huh? I offer this merely as a suggestion.

Thank you for assuming the assignments you have assumed. Thank you for coming as volunteers. Yours is a great role in the days before you. Yours is a role of great strength. On behalf of all ones here, I salute you.

Could you tell us about the connection between the ETs and the Illuminati?

JOKHYM Greetings in the Light of the Radiant One. ...Let us look at the structure of the Illuminati, so that you will have an understanding of it.

There are the "magic" number of 13 families who make up the core that is the Illuminati upon your plane. These families have no allegiance, they have no loyalty, they have no belief system except in that which is themselves and in the power, which they have and they desire to have.

Now even as I say this, recognize there are ones (ETs) from other planes of your dimension who are involved with these. And so they are not limited to your plane. This is where you come into that which is the gross beings, which are observed...

Now from these (the Illuminati) there is out another rim or another level. These are the ones that are in your banking, or your financial cartels... And from these then you have representatives in each of your countries.

Now from each one of these there is a system. The actual representatives may be as few as one or two individuals, and they have influence on your governments, on your finances, on all systems within the country -- reporting back and keeping close inter-communication with your ones in the financial areas. They have no involvement with these ones (the 13 families) for they have not the ability to get to them. In some instances they do not even know who they are. But these then they branch out and they have ones in government, in finance, in commerce, in education, in agriculture, in all phases of your life they have representatives.

Now these ones who work with individual countries feel quite powerful. And they look upon themselves as lords. But they are really rather insignificant in this situation. They see to the elected officials because they are told which ones are most beneficial for the overall plan. And you recognize this goes out to each country.

You recognize the fall of the Eastern Bloc countries from that which is known to you as the USSR. Look at what had happened, the economy had become stale. Motivation of the individuals was nil. The whole economic process, the monetary system, was doing nothing. And that which is known as the USSR and that which is known as the US had made about as much noise as they could at one another. And ones within the countries all over, not only those countries but others, were saying, "Why can't we have peace? Why must we have nuclear arms?" And there was an outcry of this -- not just a one time, but it was a continuous thing that was building from the ground. And so it was decided here (upper echelon of Illuminati), "Lets see what happens, if we can get things going -- get an economic thing going." So there was an introduction of ELF concentrations.

There were already one or two within these various countries whom were saying they wanted autonomy. They wanted to self rule. But you will note there was no disagreement when these countries decided to do this. It all happened relatively quickly within a few weeks, did it not? Why? Because the leaders in the country that is known to you as USSR were told to be quiet and let it happen because there was to be a re-shaping of the whole world finances. They had become stale. There was not the flow, there was not the indebtedness of ones.

And so there were many ones in these countries that took up banners and took up candles and they marched and they cried for freedom. And they got what they cried for but they didn't know what to do with it, after they got it. Because they did not have the finances to build the countries they desired to build. The monies were not available for them. They had lived in an economy in which there was no monetary exchange and they did not have the equipment, they did not have the technology and most of all they did not have the monies to bring the technology into their countries. So where do they get it? Right there (the Illuminati). Only

70

that is done in a very subtle way because it will go through other countries and the financial systems of other countries...

Now there are ones... who may be involved in this whole process -- and this process has become the Illuminati to most peoples -- would have many levels. If they were in this (high) level, for instance, it would be impossible for them to change or to remove themselves for they would merely be eliminated. It is quite simple. It is a very tight knit group, shall we say.

Now ones in other levels -- and here you recognize there are many levels -- and in anyone of these other levels, ones may choose to change. According to where they are in this scheme or the plan, they may do this. You may have that which is an official of one of your local banking systems who is being orchestrated by another system. And that one may decide he does not want to be involved in that any longer and he can do so. Yes, there would be grumbling etc. but it would be on a smaller scale. Where, if it was one that was in here, or here or even here (the highest levels), it would be most difficult for them to do, for simply they would be eliminated. Such a lack of allegiance or change of heart is untolerated. However if you are in that which is a different area, then sometimes you have opportunity to do so, according to what you know.

Now if you would for a moment, let us think of that which is known as your drug market. Look at this. You have within you the capability to understand what is going on. This is a monetary thing. It is a control of individuals. You are decreasing the attributes of an individual entity. It is a financial thing. The countries that are the leaders on your planet, they have no desire for this to cease. There are leaders who are very muchly involved in this whole process of the drug situation. It brings in great sums of monies.

Now where the difficulty came were when, say this is the drug cartel in a particular country -- see these ones and we shall call them little men, for they are not as big as they think they are -- but suddenly they have monies in their pocket, they have others who are fearing them, they are able to have great homes, they can import cars and they have all of these material things, that say to them, they are wealthy, and they believe it.

And so what happens is their hats get too small and they begin to think that they actually are king pins. These are the ones that quote, unquote, are allowed to be found by the governmental systems. These are the ones who are eliminated from the scene etc., because they have felt they were bigger than the system they were involved in.

Some of them do not even recognize of this system that they are involved in. They only know that there is someone else who has given them monies for goods to get them started. So this system is a blind lead system. This one does not know who this one is. Ones only are aware of those who are on the echelon above them, until they get to this financial situation and many of them had to deal with the financiers in a blind manner. They do not know the identity of the individuals they are dealing with. So it is a very well set up organization.

But now that I, shall we say, painted quite a glum picture of this one, let's look at this. Look at the good that it can do. Can you see the good of it? Can you see the focus of these individuals? Can you see what they have accomplished through focus? No, it is not what you would accomplish, but these ones are not dumb, as you would say, but they are extremely intelligent, extremely focused entities who know exactly what they want and they know how to define their steps to get it. So in unknowing, do not look at them always as the bad guys, but look at them and see what you learn from what they have done, what they can do. Not that you would do the same thing, but look at how they use their tools. They have no tool that you do not have. It is merely that they use theirs...

They are aware of the changes of the planet, because

remember we said they had these friends (ETs) that came. They have bases, they have places. They have stations outside of your earth plane. I'm sure all of you know that there is a complete underground city in that which is your neighbor that is known as Australia. It is quite a comfortable place. You could stay there for a whole lifetime and never be in any discomfort. You have gold doorknobs -- and they are for decoration, because you don't need them. They have technology that is available there that has not been experienced except in their own private dwelling places.

There are bases, if that would be the correct term, units which have been set up on the back side of your moon. There are units which have been set up on other planets. They are well aware of the meteor involvement. They are well aware of the anticipated changes. And they are prepared once they have gotten all they can from this planet to simply leave it and go to a next one and set up their system there. However, they may not have this opportunity.

What can we do to assist the planet in opposing these forces?

JOKHYM The first thing I would say to you is to put no energy into these ones. Put no energy into these ones. Put and focus your energy on being all you can be. And as our compatriots have said to you, let your voice be heard within your own country, your own nation, for that which you know are eternal truths. Work, be as a representative of peace, of balance.

These ones are currently buying up great land masses. The farming situation, the agricultural situation in that which is the United States has been quite frankly bought up by these ones. But look what is happening in that as they have taken over the lands from the individual farmers particular areas have gone through great droughts or great flooding. So that which they have acquired has been of no value. They cannot control what you would call the forces of nature. They do not have the capability to control the meteors path. They cannot stop the rain and they cannot stop the alteration in the sea levels of the planet. So they are limited. You are not limited because you recognize you are beyond the mere limitation you are enjoying at this point.

These ones have been great tools in assisting in the polishing of your planet. They have presented one aspect of a duality. The change which could have come about would have been brought about several hundred years ago on your planet. The consciousness of man dictated that these ones would grow and their whole process would grow.

So what you can do is to be all you can be each day, accepting no limitation to what you can be. And to go about putting into practice all teachings that you know, living according to the divine laws, holding all things in trust and honoring all ones. That is the greatest thing that you can do. In such an atmosphere only the highest ideals will be able to survive and anything that is less will wither and return to ashes.

What are these beings, the ETs that are helping the Illuminati, getting out of all this?

JOKHYM It is a power thing with them. They are also getting goods and they are also being given license to remove beings. The ones that are helping the Illuminati, they are having inroads into your planet, your planetary system. They are finding that they are being allowed raw deposits of goods, minerals etc., that they had not had opportunity to before. They are being allowed to remove ones, human, animal and take them to their own planets.

Are we open to anybody throughout the Universe?

JOKHYM No, indeed you are not. And do not feel that you

are, or that you are automatically a victim. For if you will take the stance of you are a victim and you can do nothing, then you are a prime candidate. But if you will take the stance that you are all you can be and you walk as you are the divinity that is within your heart, the left ventricle of your heart, then there is no thing that can touch you.

Is the Illuminati connected with a certain group of ETs?

SARNA There has been an inter-connection between these souls.

What dimension are they from?

SARNA They are from your dimension.

Were they connected previously, such as from the same planet, so that when they, the ETs, came here they had their guys already working here on this planet?

SARNA This is so, though the guys on the ground, as you would say, were not as aware. The contact originally was made through psychics, through that which was a medium-ship. And recognizing these ones that you would call the Illuminati, the Grey Men, the government behind the government, know of the power of the thought and they work very closely with those that have the ability to communicate beyond themselves.

Is there an ET base on this continent?

SARNA It is so but it is of that which is within your own dimension. Their energies are already within your dimensional parameters for indeed they are of your dimension. They have come from beyond your sphere which you know as Earth but they have come from other systems to bring this base. That which they're doing is they are setting up a network about your planet and this is part of the networking process just as there are other bases that have been built. And there have been many governments, indeed, all governments upon the face of planet Earth, have entered into a cooperative sphere with these ones in allowing that these bases be either built or be activated. For indeed, in some instances, the bases have been built by governments and have been turned over to these ones.

Why don't these ETs feel a discomfort when they are on this planet in the same way as those of you of the Ashtar Command do?

SARNA They are of your dimension. They are held within the planes of your dimension. The ones of which I am a part are beyond that which you would call the higher dimensions. The form that we use, that we have does not have the same vibrational density that yours has. Indeed, in some instances we would appear to you to be "airy" and have not a great deal of substance because we do not operate at the same vibrational frequency as you do... These ones that are within these bases, within these confines are of planes of your dimension and they have a density very similar to that which you have. Hence, they do not have the discomfort. They have particular biological needs just as you have biological needs but they do not have the discomfort of the pressure of the vibration that is your dimension...

The governments know of the Ashtar Command and they know of the other groups, such as the ETs. Why do they choose to work with the ETs rather than the Ashtar Command? Also, considering the things that are being done between our governments and the ETs why is it the Ashtar Command does not intercede more?

KEILTA Greetings, dear ones of planet Earth. ...Let us go into a small bit of what we would call background of what is going on on planet Earth. You have groups of beings who come to your planet. And one group says, "We can offer you cures, we can offer you travel, we can offer you all of these things you would desire from an inter-dimensional view. But there is one small thing that you must do, and that is to lay down your armaments and to begin to look at each other in brotherhood." Now to lay down your armaments means you will be vulnerable.

There is another group who comes and they say to you, "We can teach you how to make greater armaments. We can teach you how to control the rest of your planet. Just let us stay for a while and we can do these things. We come as your friendly brothers from stars not too distant from your own." So these ones were invited in. And those of us who said lets lay down the armaments found we had no ear bent in our direction. So these ones were given ideas for lasers, for various space vehicles, for various mutations of life upon your planet, defense systems, and I could go on and on naming these.

Well with such great advances, who wants to lay down armaments, your governments say, "Because we have more power than we have ever had. And the peoples whom we govern they really aren't too interested in what is going on as long as we make sure that they have food in their bellies and they do as well as their neighbor. So we'll keep them happy on a small scale. But meanwhile we are going to set up these other systems because these ones have said that we will be able to travel to the planets within our own sun system. Indeed they even left some ships around for us to play in. We don't know how they work yet, but we're trying."

And so, which group has your government selected to listen to? They have selected to listen to ones who speak of control, who speak of power, who speak of greed and who speak of using other ones because this is a language that they know...

By Cosmic Universal Law we cannot step in. We cannot intercede unless there are cosmic reverberations such as that which you would call a nuclear explosion. In such an event by Cosmic Law we can intercede. But because you are in the dimension of duality, because you have free will choice it is up to you how you use that choice whether you let these ones retain the positions they think they have achieved or not.

They know of us, they know how we operate, they know the philosophy and the keeping of the command, and they walk a line very close to that which would be our intervention but they do not step over that line...

It is also from these ones that ones in your governments in selected places have learned how to use the ELF (extra low frequency) waves. They have learned how to control large groups, how to incite groups of beings. Initially this was learned from those from beyond your plane, but it has been put into operation by ones in governments about your planet. Currently there are satellites that will bounce the waves back and they can be pinpointed to specific areas on your planet. This controls the behavioral pattern, this incites riots, this quiets riots. It (the ELF waves) changes the vibrational pattern within the brain waves...

Could you tell us more about mind control?

JOKHYM ...This that you would call mind control is an interesting topic. Do you know that this is used on you by your own government? Do you recognize that you have messages flashed across your television screens that are at a rate that you can pick up on a subconscious level, or shall we say, an unconscious level. For indeed, you are not consciously aware that you are picking them up. You merely know that you have a desire to eat a certain type of chip all of a sudden. Do you think the ideas sprung from your own thinking process or your own digestive juices? Indeed, it did not. It was planted there.

So the use of what you would call mind control -- and this is not an accurate statement, for each of you has the control of your mind yourself -- it is only when you grow lazy and do not try to execute the control that others are willing to step in and do your work for you...

There are messages on a higher frequency that are being sent out about your planet continuously. These are being sent by your governments as well as other governments. They are being put forth by manufacturers, those that would bring forth your goods, your produce. They are being put forth by ones that would seek to increase their own monies at your expense...

You feel you have a freedom within your government system. Indeed, the foundation of your government is one based on freedom. And yet, these freedoms have been whittled away, have been modified, have been changed, in a much greater capacity than you are aware of...

BEATRIX Greetings, beloveds. ...Control is brought about through the control of the mind and the suppression of emotion and the deterioration of the physical being and complete denial of spirituality. That's how it's done.

They (the governments) have working with them, if you will, on some level, some quite good psychics. These psychics know how to work with the energy of crystals so that specific thoughts can be projected into the crystal. The energy from the crystal can then be beamed to one of your satellites and is then brought down to cover a mass, a group, of people. How do you think your riots get started?

If you are at a specific mental level and you have an energy vibration introduced to you, you can just rise up en masse and riot against whatever. You do not even have to have a cause. But let someone say, "We will riot against this particular thought, we're all for it." And in consciousness, you can rise up to that.

This has been demonstrated in the Eastern Bloc of Europe. There were ones that decided they wanted freedom, but they didn't have the slightest idea what freedom was. But because there was such a stagnation in the monetary flow about your planet, something had to be done. And so, that was one way to get it started. And that didn't go too well so that you had that which is your Middle East crisis. You will find that that will fade, and you will have another crisis come on, because there are great sums of money which represent power, which represent control, which are to be had through arms... There is a great deal of monies, of power, which is to be had on your planet.

If you will maintain your focus and your own centering in the Light of your totality as it is connected with the Source -- that which you would call enfolding yourself in white Light, whatever term would fit for you -- the waves do not penetrate as easily.

Many times it is suggested that you would go out into the countryside. Why? Because in that space you do not have the intensity of programing which you have when you are in great groups of people. Doesn't that stand to reason? So you go out into the country and you feel better. You find you just feel better. And some of you are feeling a great, great need to move from the cities, hmm? And you can't put your finger on why. You just know you have to move from the city. It is because the intensification is becoming quite unbearable for you.

When you have particular seasons or holidays where you have groups of ones coming together, this is a great opportunity to plant specific thoughts in specific areas of your consciousness with you, from satellite. It is now hooked up that from a few stations about your earth plane, by beaming to the satellites, they can control the ELF waves which go to every place on your planet. It's quite simple...

Could you explain further about the extreme low frequency waves (ELF's)?

SARNA It is coming from your government in most instances. Predominantly, your government -- and the governments of other nations about your planet have this ability also. But your government was the first government that found they could control masses by altering the vibrational frequency about the masses.

Where do the ELF's emanate from?

SARNA There are various places about your Earth, your planet. There is one very close to where you are sitting (Sedona, AZ)...

I will tell you a story of this. As you are aware, there is, shall we call it a "country club", and this country club has a specific job. It was your year 1988. There was at this country club there were two crystals, ah so, and they met here in the middle. And they were, shall we say, pyramid in shape. And there was a substance in here (between the crystals) that would look as a metallic substance. And thought patterns could be concentrated at this point of this crystal and it would radiate through, gather magnitude, cause this (metallic substance) to vibrate which would set up a vibration within this crystal which would send out specific waves. These could then be translated into radio waves or a type of radio wave. These would be the same as your ELF.

At that particular year in this "country club" there was a shield (dome) that was put over this apparatus, recognizing psychics are the ones that were used to put this into operation for it is their thought that is going forth. In that year there was a screen that was put over this and the thought that was going forth was not being translated into these extra low waves but was bouncing back into the crystals. It was very inconvenient for the ones that were involved. Indeed, it was

81

very displeasing for them... But then when that was shut down, they had to start an experiment. And beloved man turned things around. When he did he found that not only could he send out thoughts in one direction but he could send them out (in many directions) and he was very pleased with himself. But the intensity is not as great as it was when it was specifically focused. At this point, he is happy with a wider band and less intensity...

The ELF is the low frequency. This is the one that is brought about. Your government is working on this going to your satellites and bouncing back.

Is this felt on an emotional or mental level?

SARNA Both. You can feel it on many levels.

Who put the "dome" in place?

SARNA There was help from the ground and from above that the dome was placed, because it was necessary.

If the government turned the crystal pyramid upside down, then apparently they found a way to destroy the dome?

SARNA The dome was put there and it was not put as something that would be a permanent thing but it was there for a specific period, for a specific activity. But it was there sufficiently that it created an unbalance for the ones who are working beneath it. All it did was as a shield that reflected back that which was sent out.

You go to psychics, to seers, to these ones to learn. Recognize you do not have the corner on the market. Do you know that your government has planes in which they use crystalline energy? Do you know that they work with ones in learning to focus and control that they would one day power ships?..

These ones that you would call your bad guys are much more focused than you are and they have much more of a purpose. And where you would be able to focus for three seconds and hold a thought for three seconds before your mind would begin to wander, these ones have worked with themselves that they would hold a thought for hour upon hour. They have trained themselves, they have trained themselves. These are Earth men and there are techniques that they have learned from ones that are beyond your planet... They're aware what they're doing, probably more so than you are.

Can you tell us more about one of the satellites that is being used for receiving and transmitting these waves?

SARNA ...There is a device which has been activated upon your planet which would look to be as a large sphere, or globe, with various points coming out from it. This is an -- and I am searching for a word -- it alterates energy patterns; it does not alterate intensity and it does not alterate frequency, but it does alter the pattern of energy. And this is being worked with in certain parts of your world. Hence, some of you are feeling a great intensity as you would come close to your televisions. Some of you are noticing that there is a great singing on your lines as you would speak in your telephone.

This is not what we are talking about when we talk about an energy infusion. Please understand that. This is a manmade, third dimensional activity which is going on at this time. And some of you are feeling great reactions from the bombardment of these energies.

You will note as you would go along your roadways and you would go under the large power systems, that suddenly you hear and experience the singing of the energy on those lines in an intensity which you had not experienced before, hmm?

Please, those of you who have crystals, those of you who have particular gemstones which you have a very strong attachment to, may I urge you to please, to cleanse these. Wash them. Dry them in a soft cloth. And if at all possible, place them in direct sunlight away from any electrical, or your telephone, or any kinds of lines, that they may dry. They are collecting these energies.

Are you talking about stones that we are working with, or just in the jewelry we wear?

SARNA Principally in your jewelry. But those of you who have large clusters of crystals that you would sit about your homes, these energies are being attracted and stored in these stones. So it can bring about an unbalance for you...

My suggestion to you would be to clean them every three days. ("With what?") Soap and water and sunshine. And again, invoke your own power. Remove all unbalances from them yourselves. But there are those who are new ones along their paths, and they would take the stone and they would hold it, and it would be a most beautiful experience for them, hmm? These stones are being charged as a control mechanism, so use your own discretion and be careful with them. This is not to take away from the beauty of them. It is merely to say, see what is happening and so forearm yourselves.

Who developed this device?

SARNA It is the result of three governments upon your planet. You may note that which is going along in your European -- that which you call you European nations. Do I need to say more? It is bringing about a great unbalance in ones. You will also note, as this continues, there will be an increase in the unbalances individuals are experiencing -- that which are called emotional problems; that which are called psychosis; that which are called suicide attempts; the number of homicides; those who would be driving and all of a sudden would lose consciousness.

Where is the device located?

SARNA I cannot say at this time. But it is not located in your country (U.S.A.). It is not located in that which you call the United States or that which you call Canada, or that which you call Mexico. It is not located there.

What can the governments hope to gain by operating such a device?

SARNA Control.

For what purpose, though?

SARNA What purpose, you ask? Well, you don't spend enough. Perhaps the population of a certain country is not growing enough. Workers are becoming dissatisfied. Production is down. The quality of that which is produced has diminished. Ones have begun to question that which was the established principles. That's just to name a few. Control -- power.

Could it cause power outages?

SARNA If the intensity is increased this could happen, this could happen.

Is this being done by the Illuminati?

SARNA Yes, yes. This was where the concept was originally brought forth and shared, and it has since been brought into operation. And the countries involved in this receive large sums of monies...

You were speaking of a device. Earth has crystals, so will it also react to this kind of contamination that has been put out? Are there not going to be repercussions?

SARNA The repercussions have already begun. But that does not necessarily mean that the activity has been ceased. It would merely be altered. And recognize that the influence -- the illustration of that which is the crystal -- was shown as an illustration. But look at what is the energy which is coming into your television sets. Look at the energy which is coming over your phones. And some of you, have you noted that you are hearing clicks on your phones that you have not heard before? Are some of you suddenly finding that your money reports that you have sent to your government, they are being questioned, hmm?

You are not walking a path in solitude, but that which is your government knows very well what you are doing.

The Atlanteans had a similar system?

SARNA They're trying to get it right this time. They didn't get it right that time...

KEEOTA (continues regarding the device/satellite) Greetings in the Light of the Infinite Source. ...Within that which you would call your European community there has been built and placed in orbit by the kind assistance of that which is your country (U.S.A.), a satellite. From this particular satellite may be beamed those energies which can be most disruptive for the individual. This disruption, if you will, is then likened to that which is the infusion of the energies of Love, of balancing and attunement which we call the Christed energies, or the Son/Sun energies.

Now this satellite has the capacity to have its vibration picked up by all receiving objects, which can mean: Your communication systems, your media systems, your energy which you use for your lights, etc., as well as altering vibrations in the crystal/gemstone family.

This technology has been shared by ones who are not of your planet with these ones. Presently they are attempting to manipulate the frequency, range, and focus of this projection in a more finely-tuned manner than when it was first put forth. Some have said that this is a satellite for communications systems for other countries. Perhaps you might look at it that way in a broad sense.

We are closely monitoring this, and should the intensity come to the point it has impact upon the Lighted Ones in such a significant way, as deemed by the Higher Ones, we shall then put it in a non-operational mode. As long as it is merely an exploratory object without the focus and unbalance, but rather, more of a wider broadcasting of these energies so they might be picked up by your electrical transmissions, etc., we will merely watch and we will merely monitor...

This is only the beginning of this intensification process in this war which is being waged for mind control and manipulation. We urge you to be aware of this fact, and even as we bring it to your attention, to be aware there are those who have been intercepted and, in some instances, taken over by those aforementioned forces to such a position to place the "students", or those ones who would learn under them or through them, in a state of control or manipulation...

Be aware of the activity of this satellite, dear ones. Be aware of its effect upon all ones of the planet. Even as you have noticed an increase in the activities on the Ring of Fire of your planet, please be aware these shall greatly intensify, for indeed, the ones who control this satellite shall attempt to bring about some changes upon the planet -- especially that which are geophysical changes, such as your earthquakes -- in a controlled manner. As yet, they do not have that capability. However, as you already know, that capability is contained within the resources and the knowledge of ones upon the planet.

Does the "Star Wars" program have anything to do with the ETs?

SARNA That which is called "Star Wars" has been presented to you in a false way. For indeed, this is not primarily a situation or device or set of devices to prevent war upon your planet but rather it is seen more as the beginning of a situation to protect the planet from outside invasion.

And this is, though you have recently become aware of the name "Star Wars", this is not something that is new. Your government has been working on this for a number of years. And even though the thought goes out for brotherhood and you would send your satellites, or your whatever you would call them, to distant places you still are building an armor -- an armored wall about your planet.

However, those upon your planet do not recognize they do not have the knowledge. They do not have the know-how to build such a weapons system or such a protection system. For it's easily neutralized. All it takes is just one beam towards one of the satellites and it indeed inactivates the whole program. It would be quite easy to do, or that is, from our dimension it would be quite easy to do. However, those that would deal within your dimensional structure may see this thing, this body of things that are about your planet, and it might cause them to question. Recognize part of the technology that has come to your planet that has put these into place, into orbit, into operation about your planet is the technology that has been shared by that which you would call aliens. And, naturally, they would not share something that they could not neutralize if they needed to, now would they?...

Could you tell about the ones from Zeta Reticulum?

ASHTAR You have asked of that which is the Zeta Reticulum. Know that these ones are ones of your own dimensional vibration, and they are of a system which can be observed from that which is your southern hemisphere. And frequently those which are the ships which are seen within your dimension are the ships of these ones.

You have been told you have a process which you go through with the introduction, the introspection and the integration of Divine Will, into a balance with the essences of your totality, have you not? These ones have not reached the integrative process. They have not reached that place in their evolution, but they have stopped with that which is the mental capacities, or the mind control, and they are looking to you to see why you are surviving and they are not. They have come to your planet in many ways to, one, assist their own system -- their own star system -- because they are a race, if you would use that term in a general manner, which is dying out because they have not integrated, but rather, they have chosen that which is purely a mental attitude.

There have been that which have been numerous encounters with these ones upon your plane. Your governments have worked with them, and indeed, your governments recognize the technology which they brought forth, and they were most anxious for this technology. And so, they entered into some agreements with these ones. And unfortunately, the agreements affected all of the citizenry of the government without the permission of the government.

There are those who have taken on physical embodiment upon your plane in order to be vehicles for the continuation of a species which would be an interrelated species between that which is of Earth and that is of the star system. You have heard of the kidnappings and the pregnancies and all of those things. That is not my specialty, so I shall not go into great detail with that one. But the point is, ones have entered into embodiment. And though they do not have a conscious awareness of this, they have done this in order to help to save this particular system.

If rather than trying to take from these ones their technology and their advancement, if that which is the collective consciousness of mankind would work with them from their mental capacity and their ability to focus and share with them some of the experiences and the processes you have experienced in your integrative process, it would help both species to grow. However, it would seem that Man, as a collective consciousness upon planet Earth -- or that which is known to you as Earth -- has not reached this place.

Because they represent something which is unknown to the consciousness of man kind, they have brought about that which is fear. And fear puts you in a state of inertia in which you are totally immobilized, and you cannot function in your own beingness. If you could begin to recognize these interchanges without this immobilizing capacity you enter into, you would find that there could be an exchange, there could be a sharing. But because of the alteration of skin texture of that which you call older, of that which you call their great mental capacity for focus, it is not something which is easily done without advancement within your own species.

These ones do not need to be judged as a collective of that which is representative of your duality, the good guy and the bad guy, but rather, these ones need to be seen as individuals who are seeking, as you are seeking. But they are seeking in a different way. And you would grow quite weary of that when we speak of love, and of sharing, and of coming together. You begin to yawn, and you say, "Ho-hum." But it is the way it is done. That is the way it is done. It is the balancing and the integration that you can graduate from your lower portions, if you will -- I believe you call them "chakras," -- and begin to function in more of a total capacity.

Could you tell us more about why there are the medical examinations and in some cases impregnations of people of this planet, and where this fits in to the scheme of things?

EMARTUS Greetings, dear ones. ...In reply to your question, recognize that there are many phases of evolvement within the total cosmic system. There are ones that have gone to specific places within the Cosmos -- and here I try to use terms or examples that you will understand -- for specific evolvements, for specific lessons or understanding, just as you have selected to come here upon your planet as a volunteer; or perhaps you have had most of your evolvement on Venus.

There are ones about the Cosmos that are not as evolved spiritually -- the word I would use is, with feeling -- they have not been introduced to the emotion, and they do not understand this. They are a race, they are a group that are dying out because their scientific advancement has been such that it has advanced more rapidly than the individual soul advancement. They are searching cosmicly for ways to assist their mode of evolution, their race, if you will, to maintain and to grow.

Some of these ones have left the form that they were in in that particular portion of the Cosmos, and they have taken form on your planet in order to assist these others. Hence, there has been a ready and an easy communication. It is simply that once you have entered the embodiment upon your planet, there is that which is called the veil which falls for you, and they do not have recollection of their own evolvement in this other society.

They do not come as ones harmful. They do not

come as ones that would desire to take over your planet. Indeed, they are quite awed by you upon your planet. They do not understand much of what you experience, and they are trying to understand. But they do know that which would be called fear; they do know that which is called extinction, and they are striving to overcome both of these. And some have embodied upon your planet in order to assist that particular group in their evolution, in their understanding. And there have been ones that have been involved with them that are of their own race. They simply do not remember that, that they had evolved in that particular area. Hence, they are in a situation of form now that seems foreign, and they voice fear, they voice confusion, frustration, many things at the experience that they have had with these ones. This is not the intent of these ones that come.

* * * * *

We hope, after this discussion, you understand the difference between those of us of the Command and those who are not. Can you begin to see how a confusion would arise in the minds of Earth mankind? Let us hope some of that confusion has been dispersed for you.

Walk in Light, knowing it is the cloak of protection for each of you.

Sarna, out.

BRETHREN OF THE DARK ROBES

Blessings in the Light of the most Radiant One. Sarna here to continue as your coordinator. As we gather for this discussion, we acknowledge the question which many of you have put forth. It is of the ones of the dark robes and their role in your reality. Let us explore this topic. Our speakers for this time are Commanders Monka, Hatonn, Jokhym, and Ashtar. We begin with Commander Monka.

* * * * *

MONKA Greetings, ye ones of Light. ...It has come to the awareness that ones would desire to speak of that which is known to you as the Forces of the Dark Robes. These are ones that have chosen, I repeat, chosen to exist away from the Light. These are the forces that would appear to be at the opposite end of the continuum from that which is the Lord of Light.

First to begin, let us remember that at the beginning there was no dark or light. There was only that which was awakened and that which was waiting to be awakened. The gift of choice was extended to all of creation. Ones, or rather one, chose to walk a path that was not in harmony with the Divine Principle. This is the one that is known to you as the King of the Dark Robes. This one, as with all of creation, has of a purpose. You see, that which comes from the Divine Principle is neither good or bad. It simply Is. It is the receiver that determines how the gifts from Creator shall be used. If the choice is for the self and the lower instincts then that one sets themselves up to be candidates from the Dark Forces.

It is by the individual invitation that the ones of the Dark Robes enter, begin to lure, and finally to win the soul of the one that has chosen to use the gifts from Creator in such

93

a way that they do not come into their own Son-ship or attempt to attain their highest evolution. The ones of the Dark Robes seek to win by granting instant gratification, by giving to the selfish desires of the one. It is thus that the one is won over and has, "lost his soul to the devil" as you would say.

But in fairness to the total situation, the ones of the Dark Robes cannot hold one against their own will. So it is that when a soul realizes what he has committed for himself that he then begins to come back from that which is the time of darkness, his time away from the Light of the Creator. Once he has done this he is more honed and polished. He is sure of his desire to walk in the Light. He has experienced firsthand the experiences of the ones of the Dark Robes and has chosen to walk the Path of Light. He is stronger for the experience. He has grown in wisdom for he can now know the workings of the Dark Ones, and he is renewed in his desire to walk the Path.

There have been books written by ones on your plane about the Ones of the Dark Robes. There have been ones that well remember their experiences in the clutches of these wily brethren. Yes, they are brethren for they are of the Divine Creation at the beginning. They have merely chosen to walk a path that is in opposition to the one of Light. Do not ever forget that we are all brethren who are of the Divine Godhead. Was not the lesson given to you of the one that had chosen a path of selfishness and turned from it, more precious than the one that had always walked in total obedience? Each is a brother regardless of the choice...

HATONN Greetings, ladies and gentlemen. ...We shall speak of the negative ones or the Dark Brotherhood. These are our "fallen brothers". These are ones that have been of the Light but did not abide within the Laws of the Light -- the Universal Laws. Now they are bound to Earth and its vicinity. For the time in your evolvement suffice with this statement. They are bound to an area around Earth and within Earth.

Their numbers do not rapidly multiply but they "grow" by the energies that are lent to them, given to them, by you ones that choose to do so. You help them with thoughts of greed, selfishness, hate, jealousy, mistrust, fear, and all the rest of the adjectives that denote a state of the absence of Light. They grow in these and grow fat. In turn they are able to exert their influence upon ones that would receive of them. As you experience any or all of the above adjective states you open a line of communication -- set up an energy field that is open to them. They can "move in" through a state of unresolved energies as well as by negative ones.

Initially when they enter they seek to soothe and coddle you into a state of feeling of self-righteousness and elevated personal worth. They assist you readily in seeing the error of all others and the absolute righteousness of oneself. When this happens, WATCH OUT! You are well on the road to being quite susceptible to all that which they would feed you and through you. Many of Earth are so eager to feel of self-importance that when this state is reached they are overjoyed and are ready candidates for these forces. Each time that this happens the sorrow is felt throughout the Cosmos. The tears are shed sufficiently to produce a major flood on your plane.

At this point in the close of the cycle the negative forces are as busy as the Brothers of Light for this is also their last opportunity to garner additional ones, to sway ones that have for these past eons sat-upon-the-fence. They know that if they do not win ones over at this time then they shall have to wait, and the next opportunity for them for Earth shall not be. They seek to control Earth and all ones of Earth. You know that this shall not be allowed for they have had their opportunity and that opportunity is long past. It is at this close of the cycles that they are feeling the "pinch" and they are fighting and wooing with a no-holds-barred approach.

Each of you have entertained these energies at times. And each of you have in some previous incarnation been willing to dance to their merry tune. Now they are trying to call forth any and all ones that might be slightly susceptible to their music. We watch and observe these patterns on Earth. We watch and observe man's reaction as he is wooed.

I WOULD ASSURE MAN OF EARTH THAT THE SONG OF THE DARK ONES SHALL BE A SHORT TUNE AND SHALL NOT BE A LASTING ONE.

This I put forth for all ones that there shall be no doubt in any mind on Earth that God the Father-Mother does not promise one an easy road, but once the choice has been given then all comes to one to assist them on the path.

Oh my dear brothers and sisters of Earth if you could only realize that these short term riches and gems are not lasting, but merely a ploy to use you and your energies. The Dark Brotherhood does not feed you but they take from you such as a leech. The ones of the Dark Forces do not give to you but rather take from you, and deplete you of all that you are and have the potential to be...

Earth has been referred to as a little dark planet due to the negative energies around it. Could you please explain, have these energies come from God or what?

MONKA ...That which you ask needs to be known and understood by many ones. That which comes from the God Source Is. It is not negative, it is not positive. It Is. The energy that would be taken in, that nourishes your being, is.

Long ago, long ago, before any of you had form, there was that which was a great battle, and the heavens resounded at the clash of the battle, for there were ones that were of the impatient seed and they sought to alter the process, the plan that was the Divine Plan. And those which understood the Divine Plan, the elders of the Cosmos, would not allow this to be. Much of the battle took place on this little jewel that is held so carefully within the Hand. There was scarring upon this place. And there was a period in which, after the great battle that it was covered in an energy pattern that would allow it to heal, allow it to be soothed. For you might look about that where you walk now. Is there not a firmness to its face? Are there not ridges? Are there not that which you would call the mountain peaks? That which did not have form of solidness was bathed and enfolded in a blanket of energy that would allow it to heal after the battle.

So it was that ones came, but this energy blanket that was about the planet remained. For it was that there were still scars upon the planet. There were ones that came and they saw of this energy and it was more than they had experienced in all of their creation. And it gave to them a great power. And alas, they felt their power was so great that they would control that which was about the Emerauld.

And so they put forth the thought form that they would harness this land of energy that was about the Emerauld. And this they have done. And as they have harnessed it they have harnessed it in that which is "I", not in that which I Am. And each time they have said, "I, me, my, mine," up has gone this little thought form and it has latched onto a piece of energy and it has become so thick. Know you, as you would break a bone, and it would heal and there would be the scarring tissue, and that scarring tissue is harder than that which was the original bone?

And so it is now that that which is about the planet. For there was one period in the creative force for the Emerauld in which these thought forms completely shut out the Light. And it was only when ones were sent to penetrate this that Light began once again to come unto the Emerauld. Now there are great holes in this energy band, for even as this energy band was used to heal and soothe and hold the planet, so it was also, that it was a barrier against any thought form that would come forth from creation that might alter the healing process.

Now there are ones that have come from Creator Source that you would call ones of the Dark Robes. And these ones have a great, great trust that has been given to them. For it is they are the irritant, they are the polish that would bring a beauty as you are tried and you are tested. For without the balance of that which would polish you, how can you be that which is the perfection that you are? And as has been given in other councils, as you will close that which is the smaller cycle that you are entering, there shall be opportunity for these ones to again enter into the Father's House, for it is they will have served of their purpose. For they will have tested, they will have polished you, they will have put forth energy forms that have caused you to straighten and be more true, and they have put forth that which has allowed you to stand in your own Light and declare that which you are. And if it had not been for their influence, if it had not been for the trust that had been given to them, you would not come into the realization that you are a son of God.

And even as you are a son of God, so it is that these ones are, also. It is that their role is not as yours. And they will use you, but that is part of the contract, that is part of the testing, to make you more strong and more perfect. For even as there is that which is the Christos state, which is within your eye the perfect state, so it is there is that one that is at the other end of the continuum, that one which you would call Satan, which is known by many names. And does not each, as he comes forth, bring a dimension to you that assists you in making your decision towards perfection?

And there are laws by which the ones of the Dark Robes might travel, might work. And there are rules and regulations, as you would say upon your planet. And it is the Law that they shall not trespass, for they would not enter, they cannot enter if you do not allow them. They may irritate, but it is to polish you. But it is only as you would choose to allow them to enter that they might do so. And they would use your totality to woo others as well. For it is, you see, the Dark Robes cannot create. Remember that. The Dark Robes cannot create. They can merely use that which has been created. They might manifest many things that would rule, that would entice, but they cannot create. For they are not co-creators, they are testers...

How do we tell the difference of that which comes in Light and that which comes from the darkness?

HATONN ...This is a very good [question]. And might I say, the inability to know the difference quite often has gotten many eartheans in a heap of trouble. Here might I suggest that each one of you continuously and always stay enfolded in the Light.

There are various prayers of protection that you might invoke in order that you might consciously feel you are enfolded in Light. Anyone, anything, any energy form that come to any of you, ask from whence it comes. Ones of Light will give you an answer, and by here, by this, I mean they will not be offended by your question. They will stay firm in their vibration, in their energy flow for those of you that do not receive specific word instruction.

Ones of Light, ones of Truth are never offended, are never intimidated by being asked if they come in Truth and Light. Those ones that would hedge, that would not give you a satisfactory answer, those ones that come to you that cause an unsettling, a uneasiness, a question within your being from whence they come, then bless these ones and send them on their way. Do not, and dear ones, this applies to all of you, do not hesitate to ask from whence comes your instruction, your guidance, your would be teachor.

As the hours are shortened and those of the Dark Brotherhood are trying most valiantly to recruit as many as quickly as possible, they are quite busy. But recognize also ones of Light are quite busy. There are Laws by which each Brotherhood operates. And those of the Dark Forces, of the Dark Brotherhood are bound by Law that they cannot represent themselves as ones of Light when they are specifically asked, when they are challenged, shall we say.

And so if you have a question, challenge who brings forth the thought to you, the dream, the experience. That one which is Light will identify themselves by energy flow, by vibrations, by word, by pictorial manifestations, however each of you receives you guidance and instruction...

How do we cast the darkness from us?

MONKA ...Darkness hides in many of your crevices -- in impatience, in anger, in dishonesty, in untruth -- in all of those things which our brother, our Lord Sananda when he was on Earth as Jesus, all of the things that he was not. These are the darknesses that are within you. At this period in your recorded history, at this period within each of your histories, much that is of the darkness that has been within your being, within your soul's history, is coming to your surface. And indeed, this is causing a measure of great uncomfortableness for many of you. As this happens, recognize what it is. Bless this energy, this thought. Release it from you. And may I repeat, release it from you that it might be returned into the Sea of Eternity, and accept it no more. In this manner, one by one of those portions that are out of balance will be taken from you to be balanced that you might grow in your attunement and your at-one-ment with the Creative Process. Bless this one as it comes forth that you might have opportunity to release it.

MONKA (adds some thoughts on how Jesus dealt with darkness) ...Was not the one that is known to you as the Christos, the one that was Jesus, was he not tested? Did not ones come and they would come as close as he would allow them come? Indeed, they would come and they would sit at his feet and they would offer him many kingdoms. And he would see them at his feet. This close, they would come. And he would say, "No, I am that which my Father has given

100

me to be. I am Light that has come upon the darkness." And they would leave. For he would say to them, "I will hold forth my hand to you that I would share the Light given unto me by that which is my Father-Mother." And they would leave for this they could not tolerate. And perhaps they would sit upon a stone that was at a distance, or they would sit upon the branch of a tree, and they would crackle, for it is they were not comfortable.

And at first when he had this experience he was not sure. It did not frighten him, for recognize fear is an open door for dark ones. It did not frighten him but he wasn't sure what to do with them. But he knew in all ways he was enfolded, and he would enfold all ones upon the planet. And so in his honesty virtue, he would offer the Light to them. Did he not drive the demons out because these ones were not of Light?

Light is a very powerful tool. When you command the Light, you are commanding all of creation. When you call forth the Light, you are calling forth the power of creation. It is a very powerful tool. And you upon the planet, the Emerauld, you do not recognize this power, even as you would not recognize the power in the phrase, I Am. This phrase should never be followed by anything but a positive affirmation...

Are there different kinds of dark ones?

MONKA ...There are those which you might call the "Dark Forces," as you so choose to acknowledge them. There are those about the galactic systems who operate within the same dimensional parameters as you, and theirs is an evolutionary path which is more singular in purpose, where yours is more of an eclectic one. To some ones, they could be seen as dark ones, but they are not ones whom are usually referred to as the "Dark Forces." In order to see dark ones you have to acknowledge duality, do you not? So if you acknowledge duality, then you automatically have to make a judgment, do you not? And if you are busy growing on your own and walking as true a path as you can walk, then do you have time to judge others? So you have ones of dark robes, if you choose to find them.

And I will add another thought with that: There is that which is called your astral planes. And you will find some there, if you are open to communication, who like to play games, and they like to control, and they like to manipulate. When you enter into such a situation, bless them and release them, and do not get into the games. For some of them the games can become more difficult than you would choose to play...

Is there still a battle going on between Light and Dark?

MONKA ...You are quite familiar with that which is the Battle of the Light and the Dark, are you not? This has been a very well known fact upon your plane. Would I shock you, if I said to you, that no longer is Light battling Dark? That battle is no longer necessary. But it is that Dark is battling Dark. And Dark shall destroy itself. Do you understand that?

Many of you who would call yourselves New Agers take up your banners, and you put on your armor and you go forth to capture the world, do you not? And indeed, you would convince the whole world of the correct path on which to walk. There was an hour upon the face of your clock when this was necessary, that Light would make a statement. It would anchor a commitment, and it would show to others. And yet, you are now to the point in your own growth, in your own process in which you do not have to go forth to wage this mighty battle. For those who are the forces of darkness are doing quite well in keeping things stirred up among themselves.

So your energies can go to a higher vibration, if you would choose to use that term or that thought. Your energies can go not for battle, but for upliftment.

Even as I would say that, will you recognize there are those who have come from throughout the Cosmos who are warriors? You would say to me, "Would you make up your mind?" They wage not a war of Light and Dark, they wage a conceptual war. For what are you and what is your planet? What is its basis but specific concepts which have come together to draw to themselves, each concept, specific energies, to anchor and to hold, to bring into being a particular concept.

You would look at yourselves, you would see, are you not a particular concept, you who are the workers of the Light, are you not a concept? Do you not hold a concept, each one of you? And so it is, there are ones who have come to your plane who shall enter into battle with others who have taken concepts and distorted them, as they would come into manifestation or come into being -- the word "manifestation" has been so over used, I would hesitate to use this thought any longer -- but they have come, shall we say, to clean up concepts.

And perhaps we might speak of these just briefly as an illustration for you -- that is the concept of give and take. Do you know this concept? Do you like this concept? Think about this... for my question is one that will not be as you would think it is. When you would give, it is final, is it not? When you would take, it is final. It is not an exchange or a flow. It is a final act. Hence, it cuts off flow does it not? And if a thing cuts off flow, can it help you to grow? It is a simple thing.

But I would charge each of you to look at your words, at your thought behind your words so you might begin to express specifically what you mean. You would desire to grow in your totality. And yet, you have been hampered in this growth because of mis-concepts -- erroneous use of concepts -- such as the give and the take or the flow....

103

If dark devours dark, then what are we as forces of the Light to do?

JOKHYM Greetings in the Light of the Radiant One. ...It is a good question that you ask, but you already have the answers. You are intensifying the Light which Is. And then if Light Is, how can you intensify it? You are bringing it about within dimensional parameters. This is what you are doing. However, as the good Commander Monka spoke of, you are bringing about a battle to anchor concepts. Even as his illustration of give and take and flow were brought to your awareness, so it is in the battle of Light and Dark. Light can best absorb, note I said absorb, that which is Dark by becoming more finely tuned in Light. For Light to battle Dark is for Light to enter into a vibrational pattern equal to Dark, which then weakens Light and adds to the strength of darkness. Do you understand?

So what did I say to you? I said to you as you grow in your own Light you alter your vibrational pattern. As you alter your vibrational pattern so it is darkness cannot tolerate the vibration and it is dissipated. And its quickest way to be dissipated is, it gets to squabbling among itself. That seems to be a characteristic on planet Earth. Did you know that? But think about that. As you intensify your own commitment, you alter a vibrational pattern. As you alter the vibrational pattern so it is darkness cannot exist within the vibrational pattern.

ASHTAR Good evening, ladies and gentlemen. ...You would speak of the Dark Ones... You have entered the closing of one cycle and the entrance into the next. This is a precarious time. Many ones may be lost to those brothers of the darker robes because this has been the free will choice of the individual. I would urge each of you to not mourn for these ones, but recognize that they shall have opportunity to embody again in a situation similar to the one in which they have embodied now that they might again attempt their steps in evolution...

Do the negative forces have space ships?

HATONN ...No, in truth the ones of the darkness do not have space ships as we have space ships. But they do have the ability to create the illusion of ships so that ones of Earth might be confused at what they observe and at what is transpiring. Negativity creates great illusion, and as you look deeper at negativity there is nothing there but illusion.

What about satanic worship?

HATONN Earth man will worship. It is unfortunate that oft times he cannot define that which he worships. That which is known as the worship, the satanic worship, is indeed a manifestation or a worship of thought forms that are manifested by the desire to bring them forth.

You are aware of the Dark Brotherhood. You are aware of the purpose that they serve, of the role that they play in the total of creation. I shall not be so naive or so foolish as to say to you that all is of perfection and divine angels that fly around on wings, for this would be an erroneous thought that I would put forth. But rather, know that these intense thought forms that are being manifest are manifest by ones that would desire to see them manifest. In addition, there are those thought forms that are of the collective consciousness of man kind that are quite accessible to these ones that would desire to have them manifest. Hence, you have some very strange and very unbalanced activities going on...

There are those ones about your planet that would desire to do you in -- is that the word that you would use -- and they would bring forth certain mantras, though they would not call them these, and certain rituals that they would bring into play, that they would seek to unbalance you, that they would seek to disrupt you. And indeed, they would send thought forms to you that would latch on to you physically.

105

And in some instances, psychically they can deplete you.

We have said, oft times we have said, to stay enfolded in Light, and know that you are protected in the Divine Light. If you feel that you have been attacked, or you feel that one has sent a little friend to you that is not in balance, then call upon the beloved Lord Michael, and his fleet of angels that will assist you. Remember of the Violet Flame. Use of these tools that have been given to you, that you would stay as one of purity.

This is a reaction to the Light force and the intensity that is coming forth. I shall not tell you that it will pass, but I will say to you, it will pass if you will let it pass and you will not give it energy. For what is the best way that you would cut off anything? You would take its flow from it, the Divine Light.

* * * * *

We trust this has been a period of increased understanding for you just as we have learned from your shared thoughts and questions. If there were one thought we would wish to share it is the one to see of the good in all. Look for that small spark, that seed.

Sarna, out.

PREPARATION FOR PERIOD OF TRIBULATION

Salutations, beloved ones. I know you recognize my vibration, but to cast away doubt, I am Cuptan Fetogia speaking to you from the command ship of the Third Galaxy. I am, as you are aware, in the position of confidante and intermediary for your Christed One and the Inner Council Ring...

You -- that which is the collective of Earth man -- has, by his own choosing, entered into a period which could be called a period of tribulation. What does this mean? There are changes about your planet, both immediately in your near future and your distant one, so I shall not trouble you with a recapsulation of these.

Let us look first at that which is the human, the Earth man, in his collective. This period shall be one of intenseness for him.

It will first show itself as an unbalance within your physicality. Your form is going through swift changes as its vibration is altering. In this alteration there is a reaction quotient which has been anticipated. This will come about in altered eating patterns. Your digestive systems shall seem quite out of balance. Foods you have enjoyed shall suddenly have no palatability for you.

Each entity will note a change in sleep patterns, with more times of sleep in your twenty-four hour period. The mental quotient shall seem dulled, with difficulty expressing your thoughts. A loss of words shall be experienced, even though you may see the picture in your consciousness. This is because you are beginning to communicate in a fourth-dimensional manner. Thoughts do not need words for expression, clarification, or any other way. Thoughts can project a picture, its feeling, and its experience. Hence, your mental body is preparing for this stage.

Some of you will note an increase in irritability. This is already being played out or, shall we say, manifested by many ones as they react to their governing bodies. This irritability shall begin to show its face in individual relationships. There are those who would give themselves over to this period who would find they are quite isolated and alone. Patience, compassion, understanding and acceptance are key elements for this period. It is anticipated to continue through the remainder of the infusion (winter solstice, 1993) in varying degrees of intensity.

You who profess to be Working Light have the added trust of realizing what is happening and to work harmoniously with others so involved. It will appear to be a period of intense testing -- intense indeed. Why is this so? It is so because of the infusion of the Christed energies and the lack or absence of acceptance by the masses. This place within the infusion is bringing about an intensity, breaking loose those patterns which you have which are of unbalance or are not resolved. It is a period when you must look deep within yourself to come face to face with all facets of that which you are, regardless of what you would call them.

It is an intensification to expedite your personal growth. Those who would be caught in the mire of their own dross shall find they are as in quicksand, for they shall be pulled beneath the surface of their existence. Look well at yourself. May patience and tolerance within limits be your guide in your relationships. May you be as ones forewarned.

There are those who shall choose to bring to a close their life stream rather than endure and rise above this period. There are also others who shall feel a need to use violence to achieve or act out their goals. Recognize of this. Allow for this, but do not be caught within the web which would bind you to specific illustrations.

This is a most wondrous period in which you may

108

practice your focus and maintain in your center in an un-balanced situation. Tune well to your form, your vehicle, as to what you would eat. Take in many many liquids to wash, to cleanse, and to assist in allowing a balancing for you. Recognize you can be depleted in a group, so allow for your own quiet, private regeneration and renewal. Do not feel you are being improper to withdraw and retreat within yourselves. Much of unsettlement lies before you...

Be at peace. I cannot give this thought to you too strongly. Be at peace. Let not the swirl about you touch you or affect you. Be as the rock, the foundation of strength and unity.

I am Cuptan Fegotia signing off.

Salu Salu Salu

JOKHYM In the radiance of the Source, I greet you. ...With your indulgence and permission, let us speak further of this which the beloved Cuptan calls the period of tribulation. As you would think over that which he has shared with you, can you begin to understand how some of your systems shall begin to fall? Can you begin to see how some of these long-established institutions shall begin to have an uncertain foundation?

Recognize, my brothers of planet Earth, when you enter a vibration which affects you as an individual, know this impacts and affects the collective with its respective pockets of interests. Can you see how ones could begin going to their healers and yet, have no healing take place? As your form is not in balance -- and here I speak of your totality, for your totality is being affected -- you will have many and varied physical reactions. Some will feel they are going blind. Others shall feel they are becoming quite mad. Still others shall be quite sure they have one of your dreaded dis-eases. And yet, your healing profession shall not be able to pinpoint the reasons for these alterations in wellbeing. Can you begin

109

to see this? I hope so.

You are also going to find you are radically modifying your diets -- not because one has advised you, but because you have learned what you like, what you need, and what your form desires. Old patterns will radically slip away, with new ones taking their place, for we would not have you to be a vacuum, would we? Because your many facets are so closely intertwined can you also see how this physical reaction will bring about mental and emotional problems as well?

You who are parents of small ones will find the small ones are indeed acting out much of what you are going through. It cannot be stressed too strongly for you to not allow yourselves to be swept up in the emotion, but rather, stand firm in that which you need, yea, require as an individual entity...

My beloved ones, during this upcoming period there shall be many ones who will seek psychiatric assistance, for indeed, they shall be quite positive they have lost their mental capacities. There shall be those who will seem to lose all reason, all logic, all conscious guidance, as they would take up weapons and kill great numbers of beings. I cannot emphasize how important or how stressful this period shall be for ones who do not center themselves in Light.

This is a period where ones of darkness may dance a dance of rejoicing because there will be many ones who will deflect from the Light and accept the guidance of ones whose intent is not pure.

JOKHYM (continues regarding "tribulation") ...As you are aware, you might look at a thought in two extreme ways. One can be on a very positive side and one can be on a very negative side. Or, as we have spoken of before, you may have too much or too little.

The word "tribulation" conjures up many images in your language. These are images of buildings falling about;

ones walking down the street and suddenly being overtaken and leaving the body; ones finding that their wealth, their earthly security, has abruptly been snatched from them. Tribulation also denotes a cleavage in friendships, in close associations; indeed, in families. It is not a word or a term which is greeted with a great deal of enthusiasm.

But let us explore this. ...In order to have change you must have friction. Always there is movement. The degree or intensity of the movement is up to the particums within the dimension. Therefore, tribulation can be that which is an accepted alteration, and thus there is truly only a minimal of uncooperative movement. Or tribulation can be that in which there is the other extreme -- the one in which the dimension, the particums of the dimension, do not accept a vibration. So therefore, at its entry there is intense reaction to its entry, and the whole dimension is thrown into that which you would call chaotic behavior at the point of the particums.

Tribulation denotes that which is the friction, if you will, which comes about as a result of infusion. In your case, the issues are those which you call Earth mankind, and their acceptance, at their most basic level, of an altered vibration for their existence. None of you -- I repeat, none of you -- were intended to go through great personal stress and woe. If this does happen it is because of an old karmic pattern you are attempting to balance.

And you would say to me, "That is well and good, my brother, but as I am in the pit don't talk to me of karma; talk to me of survival, for this is the mode in which I am operating." And it is well, for let us look at that which might be done by each of you and for each of you in the days before you.

The first thing I would suggest is to sit down wherever your dwelling place might be, close your eyes, and look within to see if you have four pillars of Light at each corner of your, shall we say, space. It does not matter how large the pillar is or how small it is. If you do not see pillars at the four corners of your space, then put them there. Put them there, knowing they are put there as a link with us, and you are defining, by the four corners, a place of balance, a place of harmony.

Now even as you have completed this, that you can see these pillars as they would move, as they would vibrate in their intensity, know that these pillars of Light are sending forth vibrations which have set up walls -- a veritable Light wall about your space. Know as long as you are within this space you are protected, you are safe, and all who would enter shall be safe also. Do this from the power within you, and let this act bring a peace to you, for two reasons: You have called forth the Light; you have given it form; and you have put into action. That is one. And the second is, you have taken initiatory steps to use your own power.

Now as you see this vibrating, living Light about your space, know also it has a doorway, and through this doorway you shall walk into spaces which are not as secure as your own haven. In this instance, before you go out, visibly, consciously don your armor, your breastplate of Light knowing that once you have stepped from the security of your space, your property, your home, your dwelling, your automobile, whatever it might be, know once you have stepped from that you have donned the armor of Light. And by wearing this armor you may go forth in any situation as one not affected by the vibrations. Yes, you shall feel them, but you shall not be affected by them.

Begin to look at your own lifestyle. Each of you might take steps to simplify your living. Simplify your food preparation. Simplify what you eat. Note, you do not need the quantity you once consumed, nor the variety. All of you will note a need for, and an increase in, the amount of fluids you consume. Where possible, begin your steps in consuming live juices of fruits and vegetables and some grasses. By this, I mean they have not gone through your various heating processes, but they are that which you have placed into the liquid state and then immediately consumed, so the amount of time between the preparation and the consumption is minimal. Look carefully at your diet, and pay very close attention to what your form is telling you.

There are some of you who shall go through a period of what you would call abnormal eating desires. Allow your form this, please, for it is needed by you.

The next suggestion I would make would be for you as an individual to sit quietly in what you would call your meditative state, and ask yourself, what else do you need to do before you assume your complete volunteer duties. What must you finish? What is hanging there just beyond your vision? And clear these matters up for yourselves, for your responses will be as different and as varied as you are and as the roles you will assume. Once that has been finished you will know you have completed a portion of your life, of this embodiment on planet Earth. Then go within yourself and ask, "What is my next step?"

There are those of you who have already taken these steps and are well on your way along your path which you have chosen as a volunteer.

See this period which would be called the period of tribulation as beginning at your Christ-Mass of your past year (1991) and continuing until and through the conclusion of the energy vibrations (winter solstice, 1993). Recognize within each of you, regardless of your dedication, of your role, of your station, each of you are having to deal with, to look at, and to account for, certain specific experiences. For as indeed the vibration within your totality is quickened, so it is, much of the dross is broken loose to come to the surface of your awareness.

There may be those of you who would feel you are not a very good person right now. There will be others of you who will feel you have lost all communicative link with those beyond your sphere. See each opportunity as that -- an opportunity to grow in your own power as you have aligned it with the Light. If it is your choice, you may see this as a most wondrous time, for know, the last, last remnants of that which you must face, which you must deal with, is coming to your awareness so you have opportunity to truly enter into that which is the state of walking Light.

All of you, regardless of your desire, has experienced and is experiencing an alteration in your vibratory frequency. This can be most uncomfortable for some of you. It can bring about a great unbalance in your form. Allow yourself that unbalance. Continue to take in ample fluids and light foods until the form has adjusted to the frequency.

Look at each issue as it presents itself to you. Look at it with eyes which are new, for they are eyes of love and they are eyes who welcome the experience so they might express in the Totality of the Oneness.

Some of you have had nagging recurring dreams which seem to haunt you. Let these thoughts come to your awareness. Let them come forth so you might see them and express the perfection you are; as you would recall them, balancing in them that which has not been balanced.

See this point of intensification for each of you as a doorway which opens, an opportunity which presents itself. Do not get caught up in the mire and the dross, but release it. Each of you should now, if you have not been doing so, begin your use of using the violet flame for cleansing and purification. Each of you should, if you have not been doing so, put forth the decree to intensify the deity within you. But of course, most of you recall this information from the beloved one who is known to you as Germain.

I would add another thought for you, and it would be one of non-interference. During this period it shall seem most obvious to you, the problems your brother is experiencing, and you no doubt would have expedient thoughts for the correction of his unbalance. I would strongly urge you to hold these thoughts within yourselves, because he needs that experience himself. If he asks for assistance, at best, give him suggestions for his own approach, for it is his experience, and it is his dross. It is not yours. This shall be most difficult for many ones -- particularly those who envision themselves as counselors and teachers of others. But most of you have already learned, the true teacher or counselor merely opens the door so the other might step through for his own experience.

You are being monitored quite carefully upon our monitors. We shall instantly be aware when you have established your beams of Light, for we shall tie into these beams to set up an energy field for each of you.

See this period through which you walk as one which brings excitement and a quickening to you, for it is the step, a mighty one, toward your own purification and assuming your own Light body. It is the mighty step that will allow you to be released from your tie with your physical form so you might travel of the Cosmos. Welcome this opportunity. See all that is going around you in their proper perspective. Do not invest yourselves in that which is being experienced upon your planet, your country, your city. Be aware of the experiences, but do not be tied to them. For in the release you gain in great strength, so you might be of benefit to greater numbers. Welcome this period, my brothers and sisters. Let yourselves be filled with joy. Welcome this period.

What about this desire some of us have to relocate?

MONKA Blessings in the Light of the most Radiant One. ...Many ones are feeling an urgency to relocate, is this not true? But they are having difficulty determining the origin of this urgency. Is it simply a desire within? Is it the still small voice? Is it a reaction to the many and varied communiques received and read? Is it a knowing of the imminence of the hour? "How can I tell?" you ask of us. "How can I tell? Or where am I to go? When am I to leave? Which direction must I pursue? I would like a definitive answer right now."

Oh, beloved brethren, if it were only that simple! Have you forgotten of the teachings we have shared with

115

you? Have you forgotten of the Law of Cause and Effect? Have you forgotten of the use of will? Have you forgotten of that which is free will choice?

We, those of us of the Command, have taken a vow that we shall not in our service to Earth mans kind, enter into the karmic pattern of Earth mans kind. We have no desire to be brought to the vibrational pattern existing on the Emerauld. We know we can be easily drawn into this pattern by over-exercising our own will over yours. It is a delicate balance we maintain. The love we experience for you upon the planet is beyond your comprehension, yet we must allow you to be free to exercise your own will, your own choices. We can but guide, anticipate the outcomes of your actions based on previous experience, and allow you to be free to do that which you have come to do. Is this not the greatest love demonstrated, to love one to the extent they can be all they need or desire to be? So we will not tell you to go here or there, unless there is a specific agreement prior to the embodiment. YOU HAVE CHOICE.

Any place upon the planet known to you as Earth is a safe or an unsafe place for you. If you feel a driving urge to relocate your dwelling then go to that place where you feel peace and balance. Go to that location which brings joy to your being. Know that the ones of the Hierarchy and of the Command do not desire for you to suffer or be in bondage. It is our desire for each of you to be able to open your eyes when you awaken and greet the day before you with joy, doing each act in joy, having each thought in peace, and experiencing balance as you have not experienced before. When you have a knowing or a thought of relocation, sit quietly and feel your experiences as you tune your totality to the location. Then your answer will be a definitive one.

But to continue of that which are called the safe and the unsafe places. Look at yourselves. Really look at yourselves. In seeking a safe place, what is the safety? Is it a feeling or an emotional reaction that when the world begins to rock that you shall not be in the rocking? Is it an emphasis

116

on maintaining your physical form, because you do not yet believe of your eternalness? Is it an emphasis on the material plane under the guise of spiritualism? Is it your last vestige of selfishnessism? Where is the acknowledgement of the fact, the knowing that you are eternal. You are a divine spark of the source of all being who has entered into the experience of Earth to learn to express your own divinity. YOU ARE ETERNAL!

It is suggested to each of you to raise your thoughts to the Source of All Being, expressing your gratitude for the Earth experience and asking for the expression of the Source through you in all that you think, say, do, and are. Regardless of the hour, the day, the place, the altitude, the latitude or the longitude you will be in the right place and space at the right time. You are too precious to be lost in the mass of matter into the next or new vibration. You are too precious. Each of you, regardless of location or preparation will be and are at this point exactly in the right location.

If you are in that which you consider to be unsafe, then could there be reason for that? Could you be anchoring a vibration of Light which would not be anchored if you were not there? Could you be one to minister to others in their hour of unbalance? Are you the calm within the eye of the storm? KNOW, YOU ARE SAFEST WHEN YOU HAVE RELEASED ALL TREPIDATION, ALL EARTHLY CONCERN TO BE OF THE MOMENT AND BE ALL YOU CAN BE. KNOW THIS! KNOW THIS!...

How are the Earth changes perceived by the Space Command?

MONKA There shall be great changes that will be coming about your planet. And there shall be a period in which none of you will be here upon your planet. For indeed, you shall look down and you shall see what is happening. And then you shall see the New Day. And there are those of you that will return to that which you would call home. And there are other ones of you that will return to the Emerauld for you are those who will be the seeds that would begin the New Day, who would bring about a changing. But just as there are ones each day that are taken up, that board ships, what we say is not new.

Will these changes happen in our lifetime?

MONKA This, I would say, what do you think you came for?

There has been a lot of talk about ones of us being able to balance the energies without the great Earth changes. Is this correct?

MONKA Let us speak of this. Let us speak of this, for this is something that ones perhaps would like to share in thought with.

There is that which you would call a concept. Do you know what a concept is? It is like the key thought or the idea for something. And there is an idea or there is a plan which says that the planet that you are on will move into a new consciousness. That is the basic thought. That is the concept. Now how you do that is up to you. For you have the power to affect this transition, and as you would say, until the final tick of the final second on your clock you have the ability to affect how this transition comes about. But the change in consciousness, the movement will be.

So, ones that would say, "We will project peace, we will project love and Light and we will save the planet", this is true for they are altering the planet and they are altering the consciousness that is upon the planet. And those that would say, "My world will come to an end at such an hour", this is true because this is what they have put forth. There will be a new age and a change on the Earth Mother. How it comes about shall be according to the collective consciousness upon the planet.

Now, one role that you have assumed as workers of the Light is to put into practice what you know. You know what it is to go to school and then you have a graduation process and you are kicked from the nest and you have to stand on your own little feet and you have to put into practice what you learned in school. You know that feeling. I believe you would call it panic. Your hour is that you need to put into practice what you know.

This is part of being responsible and accountable, taking your own power back and being in control of your own totality that you would walk down the street and that which you would share with all ones that you touch would be of a balance, would be of assistance. And you would be as one as you would enter into a place that you would make it better than it was when you entered. Or as you would look at the Earth Mother, can you not embrace her and hold her and help her to heal? What of that which people have dropped upon her face, that which you would call litter? Could you not pick it up as you went along that you would help her face to be more beautiful? And what of the animal of the field as it is slaughtered? What does this do to the balance of the planet?

You may affect this change. And by being all that you can be in your own totality, in your own perfection, so it is that you touch ones you don't even know, see of you. And as they would, they would say, "What is it that you have that I do not have? What is it with this one that they have a song upon their lips and this one's step is lightened? What of this one?" Or, "What of this one that when they would come into the room, there is such a peace that I experience and such a love that I feel from them? What is it that they have?" And they would come to you and they would say, "Will you teach me? Would you teach me?" And perhaps you would say to them of a book or perhaps you would say to them of a thought. Or one would say, "I see you hold this stone. Tell me of this stone. What does it do?" And you would say to

119

them, "This is one that has helped me to be what I can be. Perhaps it is now time that it helps you." This is how you bring about your change. And this is not decided until the last second on the tick of your clock. But there shall be a new day upon the planet. Even as that has been said in other lifetimes -- there shall be a new day.

I have heard about a giant object moving about in space that is big enough to block out the sun. What is it, and does it have anything to do with this period we are in?

SARNA ...There is that which is coming toward your Earth, which some have said is a comet, which some have said is a space ship. I will say that it is a coming together that has a consciousness, that will block out the sun, as you would say, for it would enter into an orbit so close to your planet that your sun would not be observable in that which would be your regular sunlight hours...

This one that is spoken of, that is known, that has the consciousness, and it has, shall we say, cruised about many of the planets within your universe and has been noted on a course with the Earth Mother, continues on its course. It is up to the consciousness, the collective consciousness of Earth mankind as to what course this planet, this comet, whatever word you would choose to use for it, would take.

The collective consciousness, as it goes into a more finely tuned vibration, emits certain patterns or energies. These energies would not be compatible for this vessel, this -- what shall we call it, you and I -- that is out there, that is out here. But as the collective consciousness would stay centered on that which is the individual and the need for power and control, it draws. So it would draw. As you have the more finely tuned vibration, there is not the drawing, but there is the pulsation that goes out because it is not limited and it is not controlled. And so the energies that go out, go out. Do you understand the difference?

120

Are you saying there is a danger to the planet if we draw it to us?

SARNA It could be rather messy, I believe would be the term you would use. There are those that would say there is a collision course. There are those that would say that this one shall come quite close to you. It is up to the consciousness.

Is there a time period on it?

SARNA Not through this channel, there would not be a time period...

Picture, if you will, as it (the collective consciousness) is centered on that which is the "I -- I need, I want, I-me-my," what do you do? You pull in, do you not? You draw things to you, do you not? And this is what is happening with this "thing" that is there. It is feeling the drawing. As the collective consciousness of the planet is raised, as it is a more finely tuned vibration, it is not (drawing in) is it? But rather, it is beginning to recognize and it goes out. As it goes out, the energy pattern is not one drawing to, but it is one that is flowing.

And so, you have been told that the consciousness of the Earth and those that are with the Earth, Earth mankind, have a great impact upon what will happen, and perhaps you have not understood why. It is because of the vibration and the energy pattern that is put forth.

But this one shall be seen within your skies within that which would be your calendar year (1989), though I understand you shall not have great headlines concerning this. It is being monitored now by your scientists most closely. There was a great sigh within your scientific community when it decided to orbit one of the planets for a while, and then there was a great in-rush of breath when it decided to leave of that planetary orbit. It is not understood, for it is beginning to be recognized that it has a consciousness.

It will not have that which would be the impact or collision that many have spoken of, but rather it will be the impact that would come with the blocking out of your sun, because it is your warming factor, it is your growing factor, it is all of those things and more that you are aware of...

We understand that the earth wobbles as it rotates, that it is unbalanced. There has been some speculation that it might turn on its axis which would be catastrophic to conditions on our planet. Would you comment on this?

SARNA ...Perhaps instead of seeing your planet having a complete reversal on its axis, see its axis moving to reach a point of stability. Now when this is done, it will bring about geophysical, as well as changes within the individuals -- those who are still upon the planet. For there shall be very few on the planet at the time of the second shift.

The third shift, there shall be more upon the planet then, for there will be some who have returned. But this will cause a change in your geophysical structure of your planet.

You think of your planet as round. It is not; it is shaped very much like an egg. It is more oblong, shall we say. But it is foreseen -- there is a 98.5% probability that there will be shiftings which occur. Most of you will not be on the planet when they occur. There are a few who are the volunteers, who have selected that they would be upon the planet at the times of change.

The third change will come after there has been a re-seeding for the planet. That's why I say there will be more. And this change will be brought about by the consciousness of that which is the collective called Earth mankind.

There is much your scientists know which they are not allowed to share. There is much they are aware of. As you would look at that which is your newspaper, you will see there was a portion of discovery of a black hole. What does

122

that mean? Your writings in your paper seem to leave this as a very confused type thing. Could this be -- and I just ask -- the place of inception for a new galaxy, for a new universe? Could this be? You like that one, hmm? Could that which is being drawn into this hole be going through a purification, a cleansing, a readiment that is going forth to form a new galaxy? Is this part of the creative process, perhaps? But yet, the way that it is portrayed, it is a frightening thing, is it not? If you get too close, whoosh, good-bye.

You see, those who travel in inter-dimensional vehicles travel on what you would call ley lines. Now these ley lines are set up with a point within your galaxy which is the origin of your galaxy. And there are various energies which go from that point that have brought about the Creation. You can call that the entry of the Divine Thought for your galaxy. And there is that which are energy lines which go in all directions from that point. And as one would navigate from one galaxy to another galaxy to another galaxy, you must know these points of origin; otherwise, how would we travel as fast as we travel, hmm?

You simply go from here into here. You get on a straight line; you get on a straight energy vibration which takes you from one point of origin to the other. Once you have gotten to that point of origin of a galactic system, then it is you may go to wherever you choose to go within the galaxy. But it is like, it is a speed train, shall we say. It is the one that does not make stops along the way. And you go from one point to the other. It is the navigational point within the galaxy which is used by all ones who are not limited, as they are within your dimension.

And there is one within your galaxy. You have a point of origin. And if you would desire to travel from one dimension to the other through that which is your own Sun system, what do you do? You don't go "out there," but you go into the Sun. That is the most expedient way to travel from one dimension to another, is to go through your Sun...

Back with the pole shift -- the ones that would be volunteers that would choose to stay, what would be the purpose in this?

SARNA They are holding a specific vibration for the planet. They are assisting ones who have had difficulty making choices. They are acting as anchors for Light. They have multiple uses.

So in order for them to do that, they would have had to have reached the level of balance and alignment, the mastery, in order to do that, would they not?

SARNA No. ("No?") They have reached the place of purity of heart, of motive. That's where they have reached. ("I'm confused.") The confusion that you have is a confusion which many ones have. They feel -- most ones feel -- if you are beyond the dimension in which you are -- the plane of the dimension of which you are -- then you automatically are more advanced; you are masters. And you are not. You must reach at least the eighth plane -- the eighth dimension, to use your words -- before you enter into mastery. You are at three, entering four.

There are those within the Fleet who are not masters, but they serve the Oneness. But they are not all masters. There are some within the Fleet who are what you might call a Lord in Action. They have attained their Christ Station; they have assumed responsibility for some part of firmament, be it a planet, be it a galaxy, be it a universe, whatever term you would use. And they have accepted the responsibility of holding the concept of perfection for that whatever. And they have become that which is a Lord, or a Law, in Action. And they have gone far beyond mastery. They have gone to that which is called the Thirteenth Dimension.

So you have within the Fleet ones from the sixth dimension through the thirteenth. So we are not all lords; we are not all masters. I am not a master. I hope to be, when Earth's portion is completed.

My question, though, is with the volunteers that would choose to stay on the planet during the shifts. It would seem that they are going to be able to go through that and stay in alignment and be saved to be of service; that they will have attained a certain level...

SARNA They will have attained a level of mastery but they are not masters in totality. But they would have attained a level of mastery. ("At least so they could keep their form in alignment.") But mastery has levels also. I am at the seventh level now. It is my desire to be at the eighth when Earth has completed her assignment.

And one can know, in their desire, what their attainment would be? You can choose that, you can work toward that?

SARNA ...You must attain balance before you can enter into mastery. This is why so oft you hear, "Balance, balance." Because you cannot enter into mastery training until you have attained balance, which means you have assumed control over your totality. And then you go through the various steps of mastery, for you have the candidate and you have the initiate, and through the various steps. And some would do this on other places within the Cosmos. Some would choose planet Earth.

But you who would desire to stay, you will be as ones who have a lot of assistance in your balancing. And there will be those of you who will go up and down also.

Back to the question asked awhile ago, a lot of us are feeling that there is a shift, too. I'm not asking you to

125

give me a date, but there are so many of us that feel that this is going to happen. We feel it in a very short period of time, in what we conceive of as our lifetime, which could be twenty-five, or one year, or whatever. And yet you said most of us would be gone, and yet so many of us that think of ourselves at least as trying to be Light Workers...

SARNA You'd be taken up. You would have been removed from the planet because of certain geophysical changes. You would have been removed from the planet; certain ones would be.

But you're talking about within this time frame, then. We're looking at the next ten or twenty years or so?

SARNA Yes. Perhaps even shorter.

We also felt there would be a major change with a large number of people going, but perceived most of it as being from the earth changes or disease, or something like that within the next few years.

SARNA And you will have some assistance in making up your minds, with some unexplained visitors -- some very large rocks.

Let me address one thing. Earth man -- the Workers of the Light -- as they have become aware of their brothers and sisters of the stars, have been most willing to go sit in the field and say, "Beam me up." And they have been very willing to come aboard the ships and accept no role for planet Earth. They seem to have forgotten they signed on to do certain things on the planet; it was the reason for the embodiment on the planet. And in doing these things, they also grow within themselves along their path of mastery.

So instead of having the focus being "When am I

126

going to get picked up?" the greatest assistance for Earth mankind is for his focus in realizing his own potential, or his own God State. If that is his focus, it expedites and makes things easier all around. I would just add that thought for all ones.

Are the geophysical changes that are going to happen, a punishment?

HATONN Greetings, my brothers, my sisters. ...They are not a punishment. It is merely that Earth is going through her own changes, her own birthing process. Earth has had this form, this particular form, for a period of time. Man has not chosen to live in harmony with this particular form for the planet. Hence, he has abused that which are the fertile soils. He has misused that which are the gifts that Mother Earth has offered up, and she is tired. This portion of her surface that is known to you is tired. Each day, each time your sun rises, there is less that can be given from the planet to those that are her inhabitants, because she has been misused. She asks for an opportunity to rest that she might rebuild that which she has stored within her, that she could support a much richer and more beautiful lifestyle for those that would be her inhabitants.

This is not a punishment for man. This is part of the total process. We would listen and we would understand that man is a fallen creature, and how terrible he is. And we hear these from many ones of yours upon your planet that would be noted lecturers and noted speakers. Indeed, man is a beautiful creature. Man, his divine essence is perfect. There are those that have chosen a particular evolutionary path. This path has been at a particular pace that was afforded to him upon the planet, and man has evolved according to that pace.

Those in the upcoming period that would choose a different pace shall go to a different place. Those that would choose to keep their eyes closed and not come into a realization of their totality will be afforded the opportunity to go to another place. For those that would choose to evolve with Mother Earth into an awareness, a dimension of greater beauty and intensity, shall also have opportunity to do so with her...

At the beginning of 1990 there was a message through another channel saying there was the potential for the first lift-off to take place that spring. Were there in fact humans that were lifted off?

HATONN ...First, why does it matter? Second, what good does it do as far as your own growth pattern is concerned? And third, if you have come as a volunteer for the planet, why are you in such a hurry to leave? Fourth, could it be possible there have been others lifted off before this date you have given?...

Each time you have that which you would call a major cataclysm or a catastrophe upon your plane, there are ones that are exchanged. There are ones that come up, and there are ones that come down -- if you would want to use that term. So any date that is given to you is a relative one based upon the assumption that all factors will continue in a specific pattern. And because you are in that which is the dimension called free will in which you have choice, you always have that elusive thing called man. He does not always play his part according to the program, shall we say.

So do not, in your earthean jargon, get hung up on dates. For indeed they shall do just that -- they will hang you. But rather may I offer the suggestion of observing the cycle and pattern of events. What is happening of the earthquake pattern upon your planet? What is happening with those which you would call the volcanoes? What is happening with your water levels? Are you watching these? Observe these.

It is in these cycles, it is in the demonstration within

the various cycles that you will see a pattern and that pattern will tell you what is happening. Do you watch the birds of the fields? Do you see the birds? Do you watch them? Can you tell of your seasons? Do you see even when you would be in your great cities, do you see of the small ones of the field? They will tell you when there is a storm that is coming.

Look at these four-legged ones you would call your pets, that which you would call your dog, the cat, the monkey -- whatever you would have. Look at these ones. They will tell you of changes, of energy levels, of alterations in energy patterns. Watch about you and then see what you experience. What do you feel?

Is this a time perhaps you note you have digestive problems? Is this a time perhaps that you find you have a pain in your head you have not had before, or perhaps in your back or your feet. See, because you, your form is tuned to your planet, to its pattern and it's vibration.

This is where your scientists put their head in the hole because they do not accept the obvious. They look for things that would be beyond the obvious to give them status of recognition. But look at the wise ones, many old ones that would live close to that which you call nature. They have great understanding. They can tell you when there is a storm coming, they can tell you when there is a vibration that is going on about your planet, and they can tell you when the vibration, the rumbling, is here and what its affects will be here.

This is the answer I would give to you, for the date is of no consequence. I will tell you there have been ones lifted and there will be other ones that will be lifted. And there will be those that will not, for their assignment has been one in which they have selected to stay with the Earth Mother through much of her change. There is a variety of ones even as each of you is unique unto yourself, so it is your role is unique. And so to say there has or there has not been lift-off -- there has been lift off and there will be lift-off. And there are sightings of ships, and there are those who ride in the ships and they are conscious of them and they have made record of this and the record is available for all to read.

But there is something that is forgotten in the heart of man in this search. You don't mind if I rave forth for a moment, do you? Man has forgotten of his portion in this. We have spoken through ones and they have not truly heard that which we have said, but rather they have heard that which is said they will be lifted up. And they have packed their belongings and they have gone into the field and they have sat and they have waited for the star to come and truly to lift them out of this misery. But as they are sitting there, what are they doing to meet part way?

For you see, no one, no thing can be lifted from your planet as long as you maintain the vibrational density that is Earth. You know that. For you must allow for the alteration in your vibrational pattern in order that you can have harmony to come forth. How do you do that? By flowing with the energy that comes to you.

The beloved Elder Statesman (Cuptan Fetogia) has spoken of that which is the infusion that is coming into the planet. Go with this infusion, let it cleanse you. Bring up all of this garbage that you have that has been sitting down there for so long that you have denied. Feed this vehicle that you have with foods that are clean, that are pure. Reclaim this vehicle that you have as the temple that it truly is. And then the vibrational pattern will not only change, the change will be accelerated and you will become more and more aware of this change. When you do this, there is no going into the field with your belongings waiting to be beamed up. For truly you come on your own and it will matter not where you are, but you will come. That which is your saying which is called the, "Beam me up, Scotty" you will find wherever you are Scotty will find you and you will be beamed up...

MONKA (continues regarding dates) ...Recognize, my dear

130

ones, it is most difficult and ofttimes quite impossible, to cor-relate the true earth dates with the dates you accept as your dates. So when we would speak of specific years there is a strong possibility they may not correspond with your current calendar. For this we apologize. At best, your calendar is several years off from its origin. That does not even take into consideration the earth calendar...

Could you please tell us of the souls of the people of Earth that are killed by natural calamities and those that are killed in acts of war, terrorist attacks, those souls that are taken abruptly?

MONKA The events that you speak of are of two different natures. The first are your elemental or those that you would call your natural events, such as your earthquakes, tidal waves, volcanic eruptions, landslides, etc. These souls are taken up, and this is not an abrupt termination for them. For once prior to their coming to Earth they were aware that their life span on Earth would end in this manner. These ones are taken up and ascend to the various levels. I would qualify my answer still farther by saying each case, each instance is as individual as the soul that is involved. This we must keep in mind.

In the event of your acts of war, of terrorism, where the life flow is abruptly terminated by another willfully and thoughtfully, this is a most traumatic experience for the soul. For this one has not had the opportunity to finish that which they had contracted to do. Indeed, many ones of that region that you would call your astral region -- that is close to the Earth -- are ones whose life flow has been terminated abrupt-ly. And they hover close to attempt to finish that which they had come to do. Or in some instances the soul experiences wounds -- I hesitate trying to find a word in your terms that would describe the battering, the casualty that the soul ex-periences. It must go through a period of healing, of balancing. It requires considerable energies in order to help

131

mend this soul whose mission was terminated most abruptly.

I would add another category for your consideration, and this is the soul that has agreed, that has come forth with a specific purpose knowing that their life flow would be abruptly taken and that it was for purpose. But they had finished that which they had come to do. Indeed as you look back at your recorded history and some of your great ones that have been assassinated, whose life flow has been taken from them, these ones have done that which they came to do. And they could accomplish no more within the physical form. And so it was by their choice that their flow was terminated at this period.

You of Earth look upon these ones that were the hand of the assassin and you condemn them. They too contracted to do that which they had come to do for they were needed. And their acts were not, are not against them for they too have played their part in the Divine Plan.

In summary, I would say that in each instance as each soul is different, as each soul is unique unto the Father's creation so does each soul react, act in its own particular way to that series of events on the earthly plane that terminate its habitat.

ALEVA (continues regarding those who transition)   Hello, hello, hello. I am Aleva. I am coming in my capacity of the official greeter, and I would greet each of you most humbly in the Light of the Radiant One. ...It has been a most busy time on the ships for we have been receiving ones in varying degrees of indoctrination, and we have been receiving ones in varying degrees of evolution. And all of them have had one beautiful thing in common, and that is their Eternal Love of the Radiant One, and the fact that they have all walked in the Light.

Many ones as they have come with us have had great revelations as the veils have fallen from them, and they have

132

seen who they were, and why they were on Earth at this hour, and why they were so abruptly lifted up from that place in which they dwelled. And we have been most joyful to have them, and there have been great reunions, and we have been all so happy to enjoy their great reunions, and to be with all of these ones that have come up. For you see many of them have been brothers and sisters that have been long from us, and they have now returned, and we are so pleased that they are back with us, and we do hope that they will get to stay for a period of time...

Would you discuss our needs regarding food?

ALMETA Greetings in the Light of the Radiant One. ...Most of you upon your planet, as you have embarked upon your journey of Light have been ones to intellectually embark upon this journey, but not recognize that as you progress that this also has a bearing on your form. You have continued to ply it with foods that are chemically treated. You have continued to ply it with unbalances and combinations of foods. You have continued to ply it with stimulants, with your tobacco products and even with your drugs.

May I offer the thought at this time, as you are feeling a physical manifestation of the input of energies, may you also consider being kind to your form. This would involve eating less of your foods at a time, having a more frequent intake of your foods, flushing your vehicle with water -- that seems to be a beverage that is foreign to many ones upon your planet.

May I suggest that you would look at the type of clothing that you wear, and take on that which is less constrictive, which allows an ease and a flow of your form without binding it and causing it discomfort. Allow it periods to rest and to recharge, rebalance.

In other words, listen to what your body is saying to you. In some instances, it is crying in anguish for it is not

133

being allowed the opportunity to keep in step with the rest of you on your spiritual journey. And you are feeling the effects of this out of balance, of this, dis-tunement that you are experiencing. So may I strongly urge that you would eat lightly, you would partake of your foods more frequently, that you would take smaller portions at one time, and you would do this on a relatively frequent basis.

Those of you that know me, have recognized the combination that I have offered to give you energy and to help you through a period, that which you would call your mid-morning or your mid-afternoon snack, which would be a small portion of cheese and a teaspoon of honey. There would be those of you upon your planet that would say you should not mix your sugars and that which is your proteins at the same time of intake. I assure you as you would do this, the energies that are shared are most compatible between the two foods. As I say, it is a small piece of cheese, that which would easily fit in a teaspoon, and a teaspoon of honey. This will give you a quick flow of energy as well as to sustain you for a period of time.

May I also suggest that you would look about you and partake of that which are your natural foods that have not been adulterated, that might be taken in simple form. For those of you that spend your hours in the kitchen, this shall cut down on the number of hours that you would spend there, if that would assist you also. You might use your extra time for quietness and for meditation. But partake simply.

Do not forget your whole grains, your sprouts, your seeds and your nuts. But look at that which would be considered a natural feast that has had a minimum of preparation, and a minimum of exposure to chemicals, to the eating process, etc. Do not try to combine great numbers or varieties of foods in one particular seating. But rather limit yourself to two or three in combination. Perhaps your seeds, your sprouts, or your whole grains and a central, simple vegetable or fruit would be adequate for one of your meals.

You will find as you progress along your path that you have less and less compatibility with your complexed dishes of foods that you have taken so freely. Indeed, those that are known as your sauces, your gravies, your combinations such as this, shall begin to sit quite heavy with you. I am sure most of you have already experienced great difficulty with your meat products, for you shall find that the meat and the meat products sit heavy with you, and indeed, they are most difficult for you to digest. And you will find that your vehicle, your body, is being attracted more and more away from these complexed foods to ones that are more easily digested.

I have mentioned briefly about your clothing. May I again underscore that which I have said, that <u>you would wear clothing that is comfortable, that is not restrictive, that allows you freedom and does not cause you a physical pain.</u> Yes, we have observed there are those of you upon your planet that would stuff yourselves into clothing to the point that you have been physically in pain.

May I use this opportunity to remind you to listen to your bodies, and listen to what they would ask of you, that they too might be allowed to come forth with the rest of you into a higher state of attunement.

KEEOTA Greetings in the Light of the Infinite Source. ...We would ask of you to remember that each bite of food that you would put in your mouth, you can ask that its energy be shared to assist others, and you can help feed your world. You can, as you would take your drink of water, ask that this would go forth to assist in quenching another's thirst, and it can be so. You have a great power within you, and your knowledge of this is most minimal. I ask of you to please share your food and your drink with ones of your planet that they might not know hunger as deeply and their thirst may not be so severe.

Can you tell us more about fluid intake?

EMARTUS Greetings, dear ones. ...You are finding that you are drinking more liquid than you were. We are advocating to ones that you drink the equivalent of ten glasses of water each day. When you first start that, you do slosh some, but it is a great cleansing mechanism for you. And it helps your form to cleanse because physically you are going through changes. You are becoming Lighter, you are becoming less dense, even though when you step on your scale you would say that's not so. You are. There is a Lightness. There is an activity that is going on within your cellular structure that is vibrating at a more finely tuned vibration than you vibrated to one year on your calendar. Hence, your form is saying to you, as it is responding to this vibration, there are certain things that it tolerates and there are certain things that it does not tolerate...

Some of you may find that you do not have the physical energy that you once had not very long ago, and you are requiring more sleep than you have required. Listen to what is going on. This is the opportunity for the form to go through its changes, and it is, in the majority of cases of you upon the planet, the only opportunity that the spirit has to go forth for education or for the work that it has come to do. For, as long as you are consciously occupied with many of your mundane tasks upon your planet, you do not allow for the freedom of your spirit for its higher evolement and achievement.

May I briefly mention also that you are coming into situations, even such as this one, in which you are meeting ones that you have not met before. You are coming into what you would call strange situations. This is an attempt to help you, to allow you to come in contact with others that have similar interests, that have similar assignments, or have activities that are interrelated with yours. You may say to me, "This is fine but I do not feel that I have some wild and wonderful assignment that is going to save the planet." Your assignment is being yourselves, the highest good that you can be, that you would be an example to others, that you would be available to assist others as they would ask for the assistance. Some are being relocated. Others feel a very strong need to stay exactly where they are.

I cannot urge, I cannot underscore sufficiently, that each should listen to their own individual guidance. The hour of you upon your planet running to others for counsel should fast be coming to a close, for you have that counsel within you and you have the ability to hear it. Just be still so you can hear it, and follow that which you would call your hunches, your feelings -- "I don't know why, I just have to do it" -- type things, if you understand what I mean.

Please tell more about what foods we should store?

SARNA ...As you would gather in your grains, your fruits, your berries, may I suggest that you would hold the rule of three pounds for each one of you for seven days. This particular formula will be one that will assist you as you would look for quantities. Your water supply should be available that you would have one gallon of water for you each of your sun times, each of your days. This cannot be stored in great quantities, it is realized. So therefore may I suggest that you would have some manner of purifying waters within your homes.

Look about at that which you consume. Begin to modify your diets to ones of basics. In earthean terms, let go of your "Twinkies". Begin to come into your natural breads, your natural cakes, your soups, your porridges that are made with your vegetables and your peas and other legumes.

There are many commodities that you have that you initially might use, and are ones that you can use for the initial period. However, as you are planning your stores, look to the future. Gather in your seeds -- and these are ones that you might sprout as well as those that you might plant. For yes, you are entering a period when it shall be necessary that you plant and you harvest. Look about your home for your medical supplies, your simple, your basic, your bandages, your antiseptics.

What articles do you use about your homes? Do you have clothing for periods of extreme cold? Do you have a way of securing water in time of drought? Do you have a way to preserve foods without the use of electricity? Do you know how to use the resources of your sun to warm you, to warm you homes, to bring about water? Do you have blankets? Is your home secure? Do you have curtains at your windows that will keep out cold winds?

Some of you have labored under the assumption that a period of deprivation, as you would call it, shall be but a very short period, then all shall return to "normal" in your earthean terms. May I advise you, dear ones, that as you are involved in the upcoming geophysical changes that you shall not have the opportunity to return to that which you were before. Consciously look at what you do and how you do it, and simplify your manner of all things. This period, which shall be a planning period for many of you, can be a period in which you can come together in your planning and learn from one another and share as you would make your preparation. Recognize there shall be many ones about your communities, about your cities that have made no advanced preparation. These ones will need your assistance.

Look about your dwelling places. What is of value to you? What do you have that will assist you? Do you have candles? Do you know how to make candles? Do you know how to make your soap? What is your method of preservation? Do you know how to preserve all fruits and vegetables? How is the best way that these might be stored for a period of many of your months? I brings these things to your attention, and as those of you that know me know I am not an alarmist, but I bring these to your attention that you might offer serious consideration in your preparatory progress.

There is much that is happening upon your plane.

There are many things that are going on on your Earth's surface that you have no knowledge or awareness of. Geophysical changes are coming about in a manifestation of one every seven days on your calendar. Some of these are reported to you, others are not. Do not be lulled into a state of unpreparedness. Do not be lulled into the state of unknowing.

Those with healing skills, with balancing energies sharpen your skills and your energies that you might be ready to assist others. Evaluate that which is within you as the individual, and how can this contribute to assist others...

I am confused at the ratio of three pounds for seven days and then the suggested preparation of several months. Would you please clarify?

SARNA Again, I stumble in that which is the jungle of your vocabulary. As you are gathering in your foodstuffs, many ones have asked, "How do I prepare, what formula would I use that I would have sufficient?" I would say if each of you would provide three pounds for each seven days then you would have sufficient foodstuffs to feed yourself for that number of days.

There have been various times given to you upon your planet. These monthly forecasts will be determined by: 1) the location on your planet, and 2) the location on your continent as well. If you have that which would be a basic six months supply of foodstuffs, and then seeds and grains that might be planted, you indeed shall be one that is well prepared. In some places upon your planet, the six month amounts would be decreased to a three month supply. But this is according to where you are on your planet. The six month supply with seeds to plant, to harvest, shall hold all ones in this upcoming period.

One concern that I would voice is many of you as you prepare for upcoming Earth changes, you are preparing for a specific number of months and then you are assuming that all will go back as it was before. This is not necessarily the truth.

Is this storing of food something that is necessary for each and all of us to do?

HATONN ...First I would say to you to go within. It is not the role of all ones to store foodstuffs. There are some of you who are feeling a great desire to store books, and there are others of you who are feeling a great desire to store foods. There are some of you who are feeling a great need to learn how to weave. And there are still others that are feeling a need to know how to sew, or make things which they have not made before. And the reason that I bring these illustrations up, each of you has an individual guidance system. Each of you has an individual thing you will do. But recognize as you do that, you come together as a group, to share the attributes of each.

There will be some of you who find you have a great need to explore the whole concept of planting. "What kind of seeds should I have? What kind should I not have? How may I get the most foods with the most nutrition out of the smallest number of seeds?" And you find you are doing studies in this.

The point is, each of you has a gift, and you will not be so isolated that the gifts of each cannot be utilized. And if, perchance, you are in a situation in which you are so isolated that you felt there is no one else in all of Creation upon your planet but you, believe me when I say to you, you would have individual guidance to be able to take in the stuffs which would assist you in your survival. At this point it is not anticipated that any ones will be in that isolated situation, but there will be groups which will be coming together. No, it is not that you necessarily will know all ones of the group initially, but it will be that ones will be attracted to each other.

Those of you who feel a need to put up foodstuffs, be practical in what you put up. Recognize you would go through several stages, would you not? And your first stage would not necessarily be to grind wheat berries. Is this not so? But you would perhaps be in a situation in which you would want to have a trusty can opener and a few cans of things which have liquid in them, which would sustain you and would sustain others, hmm?

Now your total resources, you would not want them limited to this, right? Because you would want something which you might use on a long-term situation which would feed a number of people. And so, think: What is it which is unique, which you are used to, which is part of your dietary system, which would be appropriate. Seeds, are these not complete foods? Then you have nuts, or those which you would call of that family, hmm? Can you not dry fruits and they can be stored indefinitely. What of your grains? Can't these be put up?...

There are religious organizations upon your planet which have a very good outline of what is the amount of foodstuffs, clothing, first aid, all of these things, for a six-months' supply, for a one month's supply, for a three month's, or a one-year, or a two-year supply. Explore this if you feel you have the desire to put up things.

And then let me add another thought for you: There are those of you who would sell everything they have in order to do this, hmm? What does that accomplish for you? If you have to do this, then it stands to reason that's not what you're supposed to be doing, huh? But take time to sit quietly with yourself and see what you are supposed to do, because the role of each of you is as unique as you are. There is no saying that all ones must do the same things. Take time to see what your role is. And even after you have sat in the quietness, you may find, "I still don't know what my role is," then fine. Don't put any energy into worrying about it. Perhaps your role is not even on the planet. Perhaps it is somewhere else.

Think for a moment, if you will. If tomorrow, your planet went to sleep, what's the worst thing that could happen to you? You would lose your form, hmm? You have accepted that form as a limitation. If you lost that form could you not be freer? There are those ones about your planet who are hoarding great stores. They have what you will call barns of wheat and supplies. They are not doing this to assist, but they are doing this for self-preservation. So whatever your guidance is, however you are led, recognize that whatever you have put up, it is to be shared with others. And whatever you have, if you cannot share it with others of like kind, then don't put it up because you would be creating an unbalance for yourself.

Regarding the acquisition of books, could there be a shortage of books in the future so certain ones are being led now to store them up?

HATONN You'll go through a phase in the not-too-distant future on your planet when ones of the Illuminati will desire to limit the availability of, shall we say, educational material. Hence, there will become a shortage of books. And look at it, it would make sense from their point of view. If you don't have the education and you don't know how, then you have to rely on someone else, do you not? So you will find there will become a shortage or a scarcity of materials. It will not only be that which are channeled works, but it will be a scarcity of works of your basic skills for survival.

For an illustration: Why would you buy bread in a market if you knew how to make it yourself and you had everything to make it? If you did that, then you could not be ruled by another, could you, as far as your bread consumption was concerned? But if you did not know how to make bread, you would be dependent on the bread in the market, right? And the one who has the bread in the market can determine whether they would give it to you or not, hmm? And if you went by the rules, then you could have bread. If

142

you did not go by the rules, then you could not. It is a simple thing. It is called survival. So these types of books also will be diminishing on your planet.

I do not suggest to you that you go out and buy many, many volumes but look at what you are drawn to, what is practical for you, what feels right. Music is a universal language. Would it not stand to reason, then, that as you are drawn together, one who has a gift and understanding of music, that it would be most valuable for all ones?

Could you talk to us about the idea of earth based commanders? Also, what about the setting up of Light centers on this planet?

ASHTAR Greetings, my friends, my beloved ones. ...Many ones on the planet known to you as Earth are experiencing a situation in which you are either finding out you are an "earth based" commander or you have been given a trust to establish a Light centre. In some cases you have received a combination of these thoughts.

Let us look at what is happening within the vibrational pattern of Earth. The energy vibration is changing. There is a quickening within all ones on the planet. Even the Earth Mother herself is demonstrating her own changing and acceptance of the altered vibration. Remember, this alteration to the vibrational pattern is not limited to the experiences solely of those of you with the Earth Mother and the Mother herself. When the Decree went forth -- to use your time reference -- it was to be experienced by all ones. Hence, ones who have been as sleeping were quickly awakened. Communication has been greatly facilitated inter-dimensionally.

Ones of many planes and vibrations are communicating with Earth ones, telling them what they desire. They have no hesitation to use any name, rank or title in order to facilitate the communication, and in many instances to enhance the importance of the one beyond -- to use your space reference. Those who are of the planet who are not familiar with vibrational patterns are accepting these communiques as that which is coming from the Command and from the Hierarchy.

This is one of the greatest times of discernment that you will experience upon your planet. It is for a purpose that you might sharpen your own skills, focusing on your own inner-knowing and what you feel to be truth. Do not feel you must accept any and everything, just because one claims to be of the dimensions beyond your own. Those closely tied to Earth who have left the physical form have no more under-standing of the moment than you do, and to look to them for guidance is to place your power with one who has not the capacity to lead, but is hungry for the added power boost with the resulting inflation of their ego. Remember being told that the ego remains as long as the entity is bound to the parameters of the dimension containing Earth?

Even as I share these thoughts, recognize there are ones on planet Earth who are of the Command, who have entered into embodiment with specific purposes or missions. They know who they are and they stand ready to do the mis-sion they have agreed to.

To continue with the second portion of the thought presented. The thought is of the building of Light Centres. It has been discussed with you of your own being as a Light Centre. That is the greatest centre you can create.

There are those who are led to establish centres or places of safety for growth and evolvement. These are ones, whose number is quite small, who are guided to lay the foun-dation for the communities of the New Day. These ones have knowledge in logistics, architecture, agriculture, sanita-tion, water purification, to name but a few of the skills required. No one person has all the expertise, but rather one comes and then another and another until a small group is formed who will lay the foundation for the new community.

The knowledge comes together and then the location is given or experienced. It is asked of no man to do a thing of which he is not capable of doing.

It would be urged most strongly to consider the financial ramifications of any such project before it is begun. Do not lean upon the financial institutions of your country for assistance, because their foundation is at best most tenuous. Rather, those who are to do such work will be given the funds to do the work.

Here, may I interject a thought. Many of you have entered into embodiment on the Earth to learn patience. Oft times you are given a thought, but it is one to hold for a later period. Indeed, it is to hold the concept for another time or expression.

Brothers and sisters of planet Earth, walk softly and carefully at this hour. Do not be caught upon the wave of confusion, but rather, use this period as one in which you might grow in your own discernment capabilities. Practice patience in all that you do. Know when given an assignment, you will receive a confirmation of the assignment from another source.

I leave you in the peace of the Source.

Ashtar out.

* * * * *

I would like to restate a thought shared by Commander Jokhym. Tribulation has two extremes in the duality. It can be seen as that which is an opportunity for expanded growth and rapid change or it can be seen as that which is of cataclysmic proportions with much pain and ruin. Each individual has their own set of standards for observation. Let us see tribulation as a period for rapid change. That change can be as the individual chooses.

Let all ones who read this small volume and who walk a path of Light see tribulation as the opportunity rather than

145

the cataclysm. It is a beginning, not an end. It is one step of many steps which man chooses to take in his path to his own God Source.

Sarna, out.

ADVICE AND ASSISTANCE

Good morning. Ashtar here. I greet you in the Light of the Perfect One. I see that Light in you. Let us look at what is happening on your planet and its effect on the Cosmos. The basic concept is change. Change -- that which can be brought about by the alteration of energies for either a specified or non-specified result. But regardless of the outcome, it will be different than what is being presently experienced.

There are those who would say that the cosmic infusion of the past five years on your calender are an alteration in energy vibration for a resultant alteration in man. This is an accurate statement. There are also ones who would attempt to alter energy vibrations effecting others for their own advantage. An illustration of this is the satellite which circles your planet emitting vibrations controlled by specific ones on your planet. The plan of this satellite is not to bring harmony and expanded awareness in the growth of the individual, but to cause a disruption in his personal vibrational pattern so as to bring a confusion and dis-harmony within a specific group of peoples in specific areas of the planet. Various examples of this activity can be observed throughout the entire surface of your planet. Nevertheless, it is change -- an alteration in vibrational pattern of energy flow. There has been much given regarding this activity.

Let us now look at that which is less defined, the cosmic infusion of the past five of your earth years. As you know, energy is. It operates in a specific vibrational pattern. All who are compatible with that pattern are brought forth in it. Those who are not do not exist in it. It is the Law of Attraction in its purest sense. In this definition, energy is not good or bad or at any point in between. Energy simply is. It is up to the conscious containing vehicles within the vibration to determine its use. The "value" of good or bad is determined by the same conscious containing ones within that pattern. Please notice, I have not spoken of the deity of the being yet.

If there is no value system within a vibrational pattern for specific ones then there is no "good or bad" within a specific experience. It is merely noted as an experience which in most cases has been brought about by an alteration of the vibrational pattern either without or within the individual being. It is change without value. The value of a specific alteration of energy pattern is determined by the conscious containing unit in the pattern. Regardless of the interpreted value which is subjective, there has been a change.

Each of you as you read my words have changed from the point you have picked up this document until now. Merely by being in a vibration you are allowing change. Change is necessary for harmony to be maintained in energy patterns. Change is the key to having an experience. The experience comes to you, to assist you in moving from one set of vibrations to another. It's purpose is to give each of you the opportunity to express the deity within yourselves, thus bringing about a greater change just from having the experience. The energy vibration is continued in its alteration by you as you express the deity within yourselves, or some degree of it. When you do express in such a manner, it is that the vibration scale goes from four to nine, or some point along the arc of being.

Regardless, by your expression in response to the experience, you bring about alteration to the energy vibration. Each time or opportunity allows for you to alter the vibration. As you do this, so it is that you then draw to you other experiences for the deity expression or whatever expression you consciously select to express. Regardless, there is change.

Because the Cosmos is constantly moving, there is always an alteration in vibrational patterns so there is always change. Nothing within the Cosmos is static. All is in a state of change. It has no value along your continuum of good and bad, it merely is happening according to Universal Law. The value of the alteration is placed upon it by the consciousness within the parameters of the alteration. Value is determined in most instances by the collective consciousness held within specific parameters. This can be illustrated by the collective consciousness of earth's inhabitants. Through this collective, specific values are determined.

As avatars or teachors enter the vibration, so it is that they impact upon the collective. Theirs is not the sole purpose of altering the vibrational patterns, but rather to assist the collective in understanding how they impact upon the vibrational pattern with resulting change.

As you reflect upon the great teachors who have come to your planet, you will note, they have not been in harmony with the vibration of the planet. They have taught, if you will, a new set of values. They have brought concepts to the collective which would guarantee change -- change in behavior as well as thinking. They have remained with the collective until such point as the collective could no longer tolerate the alteration in the vibrational change. It was at that point the collective consciousness removed them from their midst. It was only after a period in which the collective could grow accustomed to the change in vibration, the teachings of the avatar or great one could be made available to the total collective.

Those who had no contact with the teachor had determined the acceptability of the alteration he brought. Thus the energy incompatibility was lessened. The teachings could be shared in a wider circle as the compatibility increased. The energy pattern alteration also awakened within others the thoughts of control. Control could be extended to those who were compatible with the vibrational pattern of the teachor merely by using that pattern. Has this not been exemplified by the ones known as Christians and Muslims?

The teachings -- alteration in vibrational pattern and parameters -- have continually been interrupted by ones of the "church" to tell others what they should and should not do. Many of your Islamic fundamentalists now are engaged in a holy war, for the leaders experience this alteration in vibration as a threat to their survival. Are not the fundamentalist Christians doing the same? In the desire for control and its manipulation, the original teachings of the great one are given to the populace only through an interpreter. This one is called by you as a member of the clergy. In many instances the clergy then alters the teachings to suit their own purpose or the purpose exemplified by their own philosophy. This also impacts and changes the vibrational pattern. Thus you have an up and down pattern resembling mountain peaks and valley. Is it no wonder the people of your planet constantly feel a tugging, and they are not sure where they are?

Each change, each vibration is given a value by ones in the collective. In most instances it is by ones who hold positions such as your clergy or rulers. The common man is taught how to think, what to think, and what value a specific thought is to have. This is accomplished by the manipulation of energy vibrations. This manipulation is in most instances brought about by the thinking of man or the conscious holding vehicle on the planet. Thus there is a direct relationship -- energy vibration alteration = change = altered value definition.

It is to those who desire to rise above the uppermost limits of their existing vibrational pattern that this lesson is shared. You have impact upon the collective. You can change the pattern of value given to the vibrational pattern. You have the capability to receive and transmit in a purity, without interpretation. You are anchoring the energy infusion to allow the remainder of mankind upon planet Earth to accustomize themselves to the vibrational alteration. You are saying to the collective, "It is alright, yea it is necessary, to release existing parameters and go forth to establish and accept new ones." You are interpreting the value for this infusion. You are showing all others its value. You are the holding points for this infusion.

Even as I began this discussion, I said that energy has no specific value system, but the values placed upon specific vibrations is determined by those in the vibrations. So it is with this infusion. Much of the collective consciousness of man of Earth has felt of the infusion and he has reacted to it, drop by drop. This is evidenced on a daily basis for you as you read your papers or listen to your media reports. You are holding new parameters for those who desire to take a slower path, one less direct. This is true not only for ones on planet Earth, but for ones throughout the Cosmos.

Each of us assists others as they are ready for our assistance. Even as we are points of acceptance, we hold within ourselves the vibrational pattern until others are ready and willing to accept it for themselves. You have been referred to as transformers or transmitters. Could you not be generators, waiting for another to activate the switch that you can allow a flow of energy to come forth? Could you not be the generator holding the potential for great change because of great release at the appointed time?

Do you place a value upon that which is given? No. Your role is to allow each to reach their own value as they are ready. Anything else is but a transference of a subjective thought. To expand your process, recognize that which is experienced on the face of the planet known to you as Earth, is felt throughout the Cosmos. Because each atom is in contact with each other atom, there is a communication system going on at the core of your existence. Because all is energy, one portion cannot happen or exist without the other portions. Each knows of the activity or movement of the other. Nothing is separate. All is interrelated.

Quite literally, any alteration in movement on planet Earth is experienced within the ships of my command. Just as that which is altered within the ships is experienced on

Earth and all parts of the Cosmos. You have but to let yourselves acknowledge this awareness to experience it. Those
of you who feel as the Earth Mother feels have attuned yourselves to her vibration. You have acknowledged your own
awareness in this area as you focus on it. Let that expand to
be a cosmic awareness.

In conclusion, understand all is moving, is intercon-
nected, impacting, and changing. Value is subjective,
dependent upon the experience and motive of the individual.
Grow and expand your awareness of vibrational patterns and
their parameters. Release subjective values to allow.

I bless each of you and hold you in the Light of the
most Radiant One.

Ashtar, out.

Salu Salu Salu

* * * * *

Greetings in the Light of the Radiant One. I am Ashtar. There is that which is evolving on planet Earth among
the workers in the Light -- it is a situation which is of utmost
concern to us of the Fleet. It is quite simply, many ones are
elevating members of the Fleet into positions of worship.
They are looking to us as gods coming to save the planet.
This is a most erroneous concept. They seek to share our
thoughts rather than to hear the words of the ones who have
walked upon their plane and have attained the status of
Masters of the Hierarchy. They do not see themselves in the
role of personal growth, but rather see us as the possibility
for instant immortality. Many ones are looking for missions
that will give them recognition and importance among their
peers. They see their identification with us as a status symbol upon the planet and with the workers of the Light. This is
a most grievous situation.

As the Christed vibrations coming to planet Earth are
experienced by various ones, their interpretation is one of
ego. Workers of the Light, you have been told of this period.

You have been told of the sorting and the possibility of involvement by the negative ones to woo and sway. The negative ones do not always have to be an energy external to you, but they can be those latent energies lying deep within the individual which are rising to the surface in order to be exposed and released. These are trying times for all ones upon the planet.

There is much happening on your planet... Man continues to elevate himself at the expense of his brother. Ecologically, your planet is in dire condition. Resources are being used and abused for the profit of the individual with no regard for the balance of the planet. Ones are accumulating masses of wealth while others starve. Infants have no nourishment and die because their mothers have not had the nutrition to sustain them during the birthing process.

Let us look at what this vibration of energies which began at the Christ-Mass of your year 1988. These vibrations are the vibrations of the Christed station. These are the vibrations to assist a sleeping race, Earth man, to awaken to his potential as the representatives of the Source of All on planet Earth. These vibrations do cause an unbalance within each individual. Old patterns are coming to the surface which have been long forgotten or ignored. Individuals must deal with all of their imbalances in order to cleanse themselves for the maintenance of the Perfection.

You were told these would not be easy times for the ones of planet Earth. You, as the workers of the Light, were told of the necessity to remain steadfast and true. You were alerted to the alteration in vibration and its possibilities. You in many instances have taken the introduction of these vibrations and have used them not as the tool they are, but as a tool for self elevation and recognition. You are turning against one another, taking sides in wars which are non-existent. You are seeking to elevate yourselves as individuals at the expense of your brothers. You are seeking to establish territories and empires. That which has been shared has again been turned to be used in a manner in which it was not intended. We cry for you.

Yes, our hearts are heavy as we receive the thoughts of many of the workers of the Light. Where is the service? Where is the love? Where is the recognition of the equality in brotherhood? Where is the Christ which is indwelling in each of you?

You look to us as a pseudo-religion, one of novelty and relief. We can offer no novelty. We can give no relief. We can only assist as you are ready for the assistance. By Universal Law we cannot enter into your pattern of existence without taking on the consequences of that existence. That means, we cannot enter into your way of life without taking on the karma of that type of life. We ask of no man his adoration. We ask of all men their love, their recognition of brotherhood.

Ones from spaces beyond yours come and they would do that which would discredit those of the Fleet and the Forces of Light. They would represent themselves as the only vibration beyond that of planet Earth. This is erroneous. They seek to enslave the people of your planet. In some instances, they work with those of your planet to enslave for the benefit of the involved eartheans and their extraterrestrial cohorts.

We seek no involvement with the Earth man which is not for his highest good and to the glory of the Source of Creation. We recognize there are many names and avenues used by Earth man leading to the recognition of the Supreme Deity, the Source. We have no desire to be an avenue to the worship. We maintain always our focus on the Central Source. We ask of our brothers and sisters on planet Earth that they do the same. We serve as brothers who have walked a pathe similar to yours.

Some of us have walked on your planet in the form of man. We know of the experiences, the choices which must be made in order to rise above the mortality you have acknowledged. We are not gods, we are brothers who hold forth their hand in assistance. We serve always under the guidance of the Christed One, Sananda. We serve with the Masters of the Hierarchy. In all ways, we bow to their wisdom and evolvement.

We cannot come to release you from that which you have created. We can stand by until the hour when through love of brother and love of the Christ within yourselves you have altered your own vibrations to the place where there is a degree of compatibility with ours. We, as your brothers, desire for you to lay aside your pettiness, your ego and your need for self gratification to accept the pathe of Light and walk it in Truth.

Brothers and sisters on planet Earth, the hour shortens. Even as it shortens so does it intensify. This is a period of sorting and sifting. Will you choose by your own free will the pathe of Light? How will you be sorted? The choice is yours.

I am your brother who serves of the Radiance of the Source. I serve always under the Perfect One, the Christ. Long was my search for this One who I humbly serve. Long did I strive to be as one worthy to lift my hand to Him. Great was and is the joy which is mine as He held forth his hand to me and asked me to come to walk with Him. I pledge of my service under this one's guidance until there is that when I should no longer be needed.

I would travel of all universes to bring forth Light and see it maintained by its peoples of the many spheres and spaces. Truly, my commitment is to that which Earth man calls the Lord God of Totality. Truly with all my heart do I serve of this one who is the Christ. Humbly, I ask He teach me so I too might walk the pathe of service more completely, more perfectly until one day He might hold forth His hand and bid me enter into the State of Perfection.

Man on planet Earth calls many ones by the title of Master. I walk with The Master and I learn of His ways. I walk with the ones who are called the chohans and I learn of

155

their ways. These ones walk softly that no thought is disturbed, yet by their presence they disrupt the stagnant and cause the beauty to come forth. They lay aside their need for recognition by the masses that they might be known by one man. They see of the hunger and feed. They feel of the thirst and offer drink. Their garments may be varied, yet the Light which is within them casts a glow which cannot be denied. Yet, many who seek of them see them not for they seek of the glory they represent, not of the holiness of being. These ones walk simply, yet in their simplicity is their greatness for their greatness is their being. Love cannot be defined upon the level in which they walk. It can only be experienced by their touch. Each opportunity which presents itself to be with these great ones, is an opportunity to expand the Light given me to Be.

Yes, I too am Lord of a distant place, but may I grow in all I have been given to Be by being with these ones of greatness. I know I have not reached the plane of my inward desire for I am not satisfied with that which I claim to be. I will learn from these ones who walk with the Christ. I will serve of the Christ until I too may enter with him in Oneness. No task is too small or too large that cannot give me an experience to express the perfection within me. No task is too small or too large when The Master asks it of me. I will carry my trust for the Light. I will assist all who seek to find the Light within themselves even as The Master has shown it to me.

I Am Ashtar.

* * * * *

Greetings in the Light of the Source, Ashtar here. ...Please note the vibration which you read this communique. Note the vibration. There are many ones who at this hour are saying they have a communique with me. They do not. There are those about your plane who would be most willing to impersonate me. They would desire to gain in their own recognition and elevation of self esteem.

Yes, in your astral and lower heavens and in the less evolved of the galactic systems, there are those who would enjoy the communique with Earth man. They would seek to have him as a puppet for their own self gratification and amusement. I do not do this, nor do any who are affiliated with the Fleet. Our purpose is not to be soothsayer or prophet. Indeed, we can only give you a high degree of probability based on the historical pattern of your civilization. In most instances, our degree of probability is accurate. But, we do not enter into the game of fortune telling.

Because of the infusion of energies to planet Earth, those upon it and within its proximity are also receiving the infusion. Though it is pointed toward the expansion of the Christ Consciousness within the individual, recognize the energies are neutral. Ones who choose to use this same energy pattern for their own self gain or other motives may do so. This includes ones of the same vibration of Earth and its inhabitants.

Be assured we speak in truth, are willing to have our communiques challenged, and will answer your inquiries to the depth to which you can accept the answers. When there is a communique which does not meet these parameters, appears to speak in circles and can give no definitive response, seeks to manipulate or control, they do not come as a representative of the Command. Any one who would speak and use my name as their code will always, I repeat always acknowledge the allegiance of and service to the Christed One.

Just as each of you is having frequent and varied opportunities to use and develop your own discernment, so it is here is yet another way to discern. Take carefully that which is shared by others to you. Hold it. Feel of its vibration. Read it. Note your personal experience as you read it. Note your feelings as you have concluded. Does the shared material uplift or assist in your own process? Does it open to you another view of a subject? Does it expand your awareness? Most of all does it not bring up a fear reaction within you? Does it attempt to give you one more piece to go with your own understanding?

These and many more are the questions to be satisfied by you before ingesting a piece of material. Just because one who brings forth the information gives it as a communique from one of the Fleet, does not necessarily mean it is from that source. If it does not, release it.

Those of you who have recently opened to a communique beyond your own acknowledged parameters are finding you have many ones who are eager to share with you. Can the portion shared, stand up to the questions given? Do you find great detail of the earthly experience shared with no specific guidelines for your own personal growth? Does this one or these ones who enter into the communicative process with you truly serve of the Radiant Source or are they looking for ones to be dependent and to follow of them? If the answer to the latter is affirmative, then reach beyond that which you have received or select to close the door to the process. That level of communique can only lead to a path of confusion and leave you in a state of awareness more limited.

The discernment opportunities are multiple and varied. Walk softly. Think before you act. Take all within that your own awareness might work with you for your own growth and upliftment.

Ashtar, out.

Salu Salu Salu Adonai

Please talk about the energies that are being beamed from the ships?

SOLTEC Greetings and salutations. ...To speak of energies being beamed to Earth from the ships is both accurate and inaccurate, for it is that the ships are being used as tools to, indeed, beam specific energies in specific places. However, this is but a portion of that which is the total that is being ex-

158

perienced by the planet.

That which is your universe, that which is known as your solar system, your sun system, is experiencing the introduction of energy patterns that have not been experienced before in this particular portion of the Cosmos. As this is done, there are specific areas that are vibrating to these frequencies. These are relative to the position, to the role of that which has been demonstrated beneath the surface of your planet in that which you would call ages gone by. For example, the area that you are in (Sedona) is an active area.

There are that which are the ethereans, and there are those also that are involved that have a density frequency similar to your own patterns. And then there is that which is manifest to appear to be forms of density similar to that which would be those that are here. I speak these words carefully and I choose them well, for I would desire to leave no misinterpretation by any ones that are here or any ones that are outside of this room that are listening as well.

There is that which are energy patterns that are beams from the ships, but these beams are not originated in the ships, but they are bringing the cosmic energies into the machinery, if you will, for this is a term you are familiar with, and storing these that there might be concentrations that will go to specific places upon your planet.

As I am sure you are aware, there are many crystals, or crystalline structures that are scattered about your planet beneath its surface. These were crystalline structures that were brought to your planet prior to your time of Atlantis. Indeed, some of them were brought before that which would be the time known to you as Mu, or before your Earth had a solid form.

It is at this particular place within your cycle that the cosmic energies are being beamed to some of these crystalline structures that are beneath the surface of your lands, of your waters, in order to assist them in their awakening, or to assist them in a balanced awakening. For it is you recognize there has been that which are the explosions beneath your earth's surface. These have caused the activation of some of the crystalline structures in an unbalanced way. Many of the energy beams that are being utilized from specific ships are ones that are used to assist in balancing these particular crystalline structures.

Could you explain to us how the energy is beamed in? What device do you use? How does this compare to our own use of radionics?

SARNA Energies are emitted from our ships to you on Earth. These are gathered from the universal energies that are freely available to all ones. They are stored in crystalline type objects -- and the ones within this ship are from the Second and Third galaxies specifically. These substances have the ability to store universal energies in far greater quantities than the area that they cover. For example, upon your planet, one of the crystalline objects might be four inches in diameter and might weigh one pound. This crystalline substance could store energy in it ten times greater than its diameter and its weight, yet it would weigh no more and would be no larger. It would be, on your earthean terms, as a sponge, but your sponges expand as they are filled. These do not expand but rather it is a redistribution of the molecular structure that enables these crystalline objects to store the energies.

When it is determined that there shall be an energy exchange, such as that we are experiencing at this time, then energies are released to a specific area. This is done through the -- and I struggle here for a word -- shall we say, upon your plane this would be through a computer system, specific amounts of energies are released. These stimulate specific areas of your brain, bringing about an increased consciousness or awareness. This also enables you to feel specific energy patterns that heretofore you had not been aware of. And these energies are used to assist you who are receiving them to attain a higher state of awareness. These are merely projected forth from the ships through a system that is similar to that which you would call a computer system. It is determined what ratio would be shared with specific groupings in order to establish the pattern that would come forth to ones upon your planet; indeed, to ones of your circle.

At the time that I am speaking with you, I am relatively close. The ship is relatively close to Earth for I am approximately 150 miles from you. Yet I can send forth energies that are pointed specifically at this dwelling, for I have the capability upon the monitor to see the energy patterns as they are coming forth, where they are going, and indeed, to monitor the effect that they have on each one of you. It is a quite simple procedure really. And I must use my thinking power to put this in words that you would understand, for indeed this has become a natural process for me.

While in meditation I became aware of the beam that you of the Space Command surround us with during this meeting. The vision I got was that knowledge was here and it was sparking in each of us and then we were sparking each other. It was a really beautiful image that we were experiencing.

SARNA You have a great accuracy in that which you express. For those of you that perhaps do not see it, visualize a ship, a space ship if you will, several miles above you. And from the center of that ship that you can see there is as a beam -- perhaps you would call it a column of light that enfolds the area where you are.

Now this column as you would say, would be a rather unique column, for it does not allow in that which would unbalance or that which would not be for your own learning process or your highest good. Translate that in that any ELF waves that are in your area would come to the outer parameters and bounce back.

Those within your government and those with other interests are well aware of the transmission that comes through this beam. They know there is a transmission going on, but it cannot be intercepted. It cannot be altered, or tampered with. There is merely an awareness that it is going on. Indeed there is a satellite currently that is picking up and sending forth to a monitor a "ping, ping, ping" as this transmission is going forth. This is being picked up in that which you would call your (former) Soviet Union as well as that which would be called a station within one of the desert areas of your own country.

Now this beam initially cleaned and cleared your own energy patterns. You will note when you first came together there was not a balancing within yourselves or within the circle. As was told to you when last we gathered, take the number of you that is in the circle, magnify or multiply that times itself, and that is the energy that is available through you and to you.

Each of you shares of your own vibration with the others, so you would see as you say, the sparks going, the inter-connectedness going from one to the other of you. As the energy or vibration that is shared with you through the column comes to you, it sparks and activates within you a balancing and an opportunity for expanded awareness. Nothing, no thing can enter or come to you without your consent. So it is not that anything is being imposed upon you. But see if you would a line of energy much as a flash of lightening within your plane that goes about your circle and goes from one to the other. It is going clockwise and counter clockwise. So you have this situation with each of you.

In addition, you have the vibration coming to you through this beam. You could say that this column is like your air after a great thunderstorm. It is a cleared, refined area in which there can be a clarity of energy vibration come to you. And so energy is coming this way and this way. So what happens within you? You become a vortex. As you allow this experience within yourself, certain cells within your consciousness are stimulated and you awaken to a greater understanding within yourself. It is our great desire that through this experience you would maintain this vortex of energy within yourself once your circle is no longer in physical being.

Now when the Masters would speak, they do not come through this beam or this column. For indeed when the good Master T. (Theoaphylos) would speak through this one, what is experienced is an enfoldment and connection. You that have eye to see would see that there is a Light pattern that enfolds this one through which we speak. So in actuality she receives in two different ways. For when the Master T. would come, he would enfold and there would be a Light pattern that would be about her and they would share this vibration; where ours is more of a transmission and she would be a receiver even as you would be a receiver.

But if you would, in the days that are before you, each of you close your eyes and visualize yourself as this vortex that is swirling, because within this column, even though energy as you would say, "comes down" or comes to you, so it is energy is also rising. So you have many motions that are going on within you or much movement. Have not you been told that life is movement? And this is what you experience.

* * * * *

As you see from our discussion, we are very aware of the changes and feelings of ones on planet Earth. We monitor the workers of the Light most closely. It is our desire to clarify the record in this discussion, removing points of confusion and difficulty.

Go forth in peace, in love, in universal brotherhood.

Sarna, out.

LIFT-OFF

Greetings and salutations. Soltec here. ...Concerning the "date, time and place" syndrome, let us now look at it in a different way. As is stated in the Law of Attraction, you draw to you that which you desire. Even though this is done, it is not always understood consciously the reason for the drawing of the experience or thought.

Man, the collective, desires to have dates, times and places, so this is given through many ones. Man continues to see us as all knowing and as soothsayers holding the future for planet Earth in our hands. This we do not do. He, by his desires asks from us to give him dates, times and places. When this desire is put forth, it sets into motion the Law of Attraction. We then give to man a specific date or place. As man receives this within himself he then is the initiator of an alteration in his pattern of attraction. Translated -- what does he do with the thought? If the thought is used for growth such as a preparation with no fear then the thought was indeed one which was received in the highest order of man's capability. He has gleaned only balance from the thought and his pattern of attraction is so. If on the other hand he becomes quite fearful and begins to hoard or to escape from a place then he has gleaned only unbalance, thus adding to the unbalance of the planet and the collective.

Look at that which was a thought not put forth from beyond your dimension, but within your dimension concerning the New Madrid fault line. From the simple thought of a 50% chance of experience of that portion of the earth quaking, what did man do with it? Yes, there were those few who became quite excited and unbalanced, but the majority used this thought as an opportunity to practice the use of the survival methods and equipment available to man. Schools and businesses were closed so that man would not be caught indoors, but rather was with his family and the place of his greatest need for coming together. There was not a mass hysteria of evacuation of the area creating greater unbalance. Because of man's preparatory attitude he gleaned balance. He learned and from his learning he began to understand his own needs in a situation of such and its many ramifications and complexities. For this we applaud man!

Through [this one, Tuieta], we have given dates and places. Why? To afford man the opportunity to learn to be at balance even as an unbalancing thought is taken within man. Any changes about the face of your planet are changes of Light -- balance being gleaned from unbalance. All change is a blessing. It is only that man cannot see that blessing, but relies on the unbalance or the negativity of the moment thus taking to himself only unbalance. See all going on about you as an opportunity for growth in understanding on your steps to KNOWING.

Let us take one more illustration. The "Third Meeting of the Conclave" has within it specific dates as to years of probable experience for the collective known as mankind of Earth. What does man do with this thought? Is it an opportunity to produce unbalance? Is he using it to bring riches to himself? What is man doing with this thought? In most instances monitored man is using this information to prepare. He is feeling the desire to come together with groups and to share in the techniques of survival. Man is coming together with man to see their commonality rather than their differences. Man is using this information as one more morsel in his growth process. He, man, can slow down or alter the speed of change because of his own attitude as an individual. Mass fear merely draws additional unbalance to it producing still greater fear/unbalance.

Brothers and sisters of planet Earth, begin to see of your own responsibility for what is happening with you. See how in each small way, you draw to you by your thoughts and actions. If each opportunity is used for coming into a balance

165

toward your own Christ manifestation then truly you have risen beyond the limitation of DATE, TIME, and PLACE.

Soltec out.

Salu Salu Salu

How will we know to be in the right place at the right time to be beamed up?

ANDROMEDA REX I am Andromeda Rex, and I assure you, each and everyone, YOU SHALL RECEIVE YOUR SIGNAL! Do not be concerned with not receiving your direction. There will be no doubt. In the event there shall be total earthly evacuation all media channels will be taken over to broadcast our presence and our purpose. Indeed, many of you will see me and I will give you your directions. Here I speak of the mass lift-off. Those of you that are to be lifted shall be. Do not be concerned. You will have no doubt...

ANDROMEDA REX (also states) ...Many of you will have your initial contact with the Fleet by receiving my vibrations. This is part of my assignment with the Fleet because of the energy pattern that I can transmit. This is one that is easily picked up in your receivers...

At the time of lift-off, the impression that I have gotten is that the numbers that will be lifted are very, very few compared to the total Earth's population. Is this so? What about the ones that are not involved in the Light work?

MONKA Greetings, ye ones of Light. ...There have been vast interpretations of what we have given concerning the lift-off for you ones of Earth in the event that Mother Earth must be evacuated. I am sad to say that if Earth were to be evacuated this hour there would not be large numbers in

166

proportion to Earth's total population.

The criteria for evacuation from Earth by ones of the Fleet is not a long and a complicated one. You have been given the criteria repeatedly, indeed, I would say for the past 2,000 years that are within your recorded history. The criteria is love. And I do not speak of a gush and a goo. And I do not speak of an emotional reaction or a physical attraction. I speak of Divine Love -- love of the Creator as the Creator, and recognition of this One that did place All within their place. And love of thy brother and thy sister, that divine essence which is within each one that walks the Earth with you. Do not be quick to judge or condemn another, for you do not know what their purpose is upon Earth at this hour. But I would say to you briefly this is the criteria. And sadly there are many, many ones upon your Earth that fall far short of this criteria.

Now there are ones that walk about your Earth that appear to be rather lackadaisical and unconcerned, but I assure you on the higher planes these ones are quite busy. I would also suggest to you that you remember or you recognize that the physical form which you now occupy is but a tool or a vehicle for your soul's progression, your divine portion, your essence. And just as you have entered into this vehicle to learn specific lessons, to do specific things to help you along your evolutionary path, so do you also leave of this vehicle to travel forth in spirit that many of you minister to others, that you go forth to learn lessons, that you do varying things that assist you along your path. Indeed many of you are not totally aware of all that you do.

Now when the hour comes that there shall be a lift-off from Mother Earth I have given you the criteria. I will also add that it will expedite one's evacuation if they are not afraid. Our purpose at coming through to varying ones on Earth with the frequency that we do, in the variety of ways that we do is to help alleviate any fear that you would have concerning us and our ships. For you see fear is a negative energy and it puts forth negative vibrations that would impede our assistance to you. No, ones do not have to be totally schooled in Light teachings to be brought forth, but one has to feel love within their heart and to be able to see of the Divine Creator in all and everyone that is about them.

They do not have to be schooled in Light techniques. They do not have to follow some specific Earth-man's teachings. They have merely to recognize from whence they came and where they are going and to say to their Creator, "Whatever is Thy Will then let it be mine." And to look to their brother or their sister and to truly say, "I love you." This is the criteria, my brother. And I am sad to say there are many, many ones on the earthly plane that choose not to meet the criteria. The choice is theirs. It is not ours. For we have the facilities to evacuate all ones of Earth should they choose to awaken.

I will also add that we have worked most diligently with Earth, and ones of Earth to give Earth man every available opportunity that he might have to awaken to his Creator, his Creation, and his Divine Purpose. For once the cycle closes Earth man then is locked into his choice as of that particular second in his time.

HATONN (adds) Greetings, ladies and gentlemen. ...There are ones that shall be lifted, there are ones that have been lifted. And there are a good number of you that are going to stay right where you are, for that is the assignment that you signed up for.

Now, I recognize that is a little disappointing, for there has been a vogue idea going about your planet, and I believe it's called, "Beam me up, Scotty." This is, if you would excuse my saying so, taking the easy way out. There will be ones of you that will come, there are ones of you now that have already been within the ships. You have lost, perhaps, a half hour. You have sat down in your chair and you have dozed off. You woke up an hour later, not realizing that you had "taken a nap". You have come for instruction, you have come for an increase in the energy ratio that you can tolerate, you have come for many reasons.

As is foreseen <u>at this point within the cycle</u> -- and may I underscore that carefully, for man has the opportunity to change this at any moment -- as is foreseen, there shall be a lift-off, but it will be done in phases, according to assignments of individuals. Those of you that have been assigned to, have selected the assignment of being here to assist during the physical changes upon the planet, shall be ones that stay for the longest period of time. Some of you will not enter the ships in physical form, but you will come in spirit. There are other ones that will come in physical form. There is no one specific formula that covers each one, for each assignment is individual, and each assignment rests upon that which is done by another, and so on.

It is anticipated at this particular place within the cycle, at the time that there is the complete changing, or cleansing, the last cleansing process that will go on within the planet, then that which is known as man kind will be briefly removed that he might return when the Earth has finished this process and she is awakening.

I have not given you the specific that you would desire, and I know this, but it is that I cannot give it to you be-cause it depends on Earth mankind. However, with your indulgence, let me again emphasize to each of you to seriously think about those unscheduled naps you have had, those dreams you have had, those times when you have lost an hour, a half hour, or fifteen minutes. As you study of these periods, brief glimpses of activity shall flash before your eyes and perhaps shall give you a clue as to what you have been doing...

SOLTEC ...Now the next question that comes with the earth changes, is what of the children, and what of the animals -- translated, "The pets that I hold near and dear". This is often asked of us as we go forth.

First the children are newly entered souls and because they are newly entered souls they are the first ones who will be evacuated. Ships have been set up to take care of the children. There are those of you whose assignment is to work upon these ships and work with the children.

Now the real surprise comes when the children come aboard the ships and you find out they are not these small inexperienced beings that you think they are. But they grow and mature very quickly into that which is the full soul consciousness. So you who are concerned of your children, have no concern or worry. They are well taken care of, they are well prepared for. And once you have been evacuated you will have an opportunity to reunite with these ones. However it will be a bit of a shocking experience, initially, because you will also be in your full soul reality, just as they are, so your reunion may be slightly different.

And now for the four legged ones, these that you call the animals, your pets, your companions, your special friends. In some instances you will find your animals will be waiting for you in your rooms. In other instances you will find they have been evacuated to a place of safety. So have no concern for these ones. Love them, even as you love them now upon your planet, but your greatest love is to release them to go or to be where they need to be. There are those of you because of bondings of previous embodiments with a particular animal, a particular bird, that you will find they are waiting for you in your room when you have boarded the ships.

When lift-off comes, is there a special place for the wild animals to go also?

JOKHYM In the radiance of the Source, I greet you. ...You speak of these small ones that have been entrusted to you upon the planet. Indeed, there is a place for these ones. You will note there are many ones that are being removed from your planet already. They are called, I believe, extinct specie. Is this what they are called? For they are being removed. And you will find those that have been ones that have been great warriors among their own kind are coming into a scarcity upon your plane that they might go to other spheres and relearn what they have learned to begin with and to help them to release that which they have learned from man. Did you know that? For where do you think they learned to kill and where did they learn to eat the flesh of one another but from their greatest teachers -- the lords that were manifest upon your plane. So, these ones are being removed.

The ones of the waters that are truly your brothers and sisters of cosmic origin (eg dolphins) too are being removed from your planet for they have finished their portion. They have worked with you in many ways and they are taking their leave for they have completed that which they have come to do, and theirs, too, shall be an exit from the planet...

One book I read mentioned that those that do not wish to board the space ships, they will be returned back to God. I didn't understand what they mean by that?

MONKA You are aware, each of you, that you have been given the Divine Gift of choice. Those of you in the final hours that choose not to accept the assistance that we offer shall be taken up within the Universal Flow. In earthly terms, they shall return to spirit. But the specific identity of the individual shall meld within the house from which they came. Thus, all that is good, and all that which they have yet to accomplish shall be balanced and negated within their house. These shall be ones that shall not come forth specifically as they are known at this time, for they shall meld into the house from whence they came.

There are specific ones upon the planet Earth that shall be lifted to return to planet Earth in the new day that they might be the ones, the elders, the elder brothers of the race that shall inhabit Earth in the next cycle. This has been determined long before you put your foot on Earth for this cycle.

There are still others, a third group, that shall be taken up from Earth, be it in spirit form or be it in a form in which they board our ships, that shall be taken to other planets, to other stars to learn specific lessons, to grow in the ethers, the environment of these places.

There are still others, a fourth group, that shall inhabit a new planet, one with which you are not familiar -- one that is similar to Earth at this time, without the conveniences that your science and your technological endeavors have given to you. These ones shall have opportunity to progress along their path at a rate that is compatible for them...

How will we be lifted off?

BEATRIX Greetings, beloveds. ...We of the Fleet at this time, or rather I should say, those of us that are particularly involved with the engineering feats of the Fleet, have been most occupied in bringing forth a beam of energy, of Light, in which you might be lifted, you might be brought within the ship, and there shall be a minimal of molecular disturbance for each of you. We shall continue to concentrate our activities in this area in the upcoming days, for our objective is for each of you to be able to come into the ships with no discomfort or unbalance in your molecular structure. It is hoped that our efforts shall be rewarded as we combine our thoughts and our energies in this common goal. Thank you for allowing me to share this thought with you.

And once aboard the ships?

ALEVA Good evening ladies and gentlemen, my name is

Aleva. For your convenience, dear ones I shall spell this. It shall be A-L-E-V-A. I am informed it is now my turn that I might speak with you. Thank you for allowing me to come forth. I would be known to you of Earth as one of the space people, though to us this does seem a strange way of referring to brothers and sisters. I have come from a distant plant that I might assist you of Earth in the days to come. It is my joy to tell you that I am responsible for a group of guides for you of Earth here on various ships. You might refer to us as "big brothers or big sisters" for we shall be with you as you come. We shall help you in your adjustment, help to answer many of your questions and to ease your transition into this dimension of our ships.

We have been assigned to groups of three to five individuals on Earth that we might help you as you take your steps from Earth to here. Just as we have been assigned to you ones we monitor your activities quite closely that we might familiarize ourselves with your preferences, your manner of speaking, your thought patterns and your "personalities" so that we might make you as comfortable as quickly as possible.

I am sure that there are many on Earth that are concerned of the eating patterns here on our ships. I am also sure that you are concerned as to the manner of dress and what to expect. As we have sat in our various councils we have come to the conclusion that it might help you if we gave you a brief summary of your initial days with us as you come forth. With your permission I should like to do this at this time.

As you come forth, as you are beamed forth, you will enter into a room that to you would be like full of equipment. You would stand there for a short time until your cellular activity has adjusted to our frequency rate. At such a time then your guide would take you into a larger room, for there shall be many that will be coming forth. This would be as you would call an entry way, a grand hall or such. In this large room you will find many with whom you are familiar. These shall be ones of Earth and ones from higher dimensions as well. This is a general mingling time and to help you acclimatize yourself to your new surroundings so that you will have no fear or apprehension. Then after a short period you will be shown to your rooms for a welcomed opportunity to refresh yourselves and rest.

During your initial period with us you shall be taken into that portion which we call our medical facilities that you might receive of balancing, that certain sleeping portions of your brain might be activated so that thought communication can quite easily be established with each of you. No, this shall alter you in no way, and have no fear that we shall attempt any mind control, though I know this has been spoken of on your planet. We do not use speech such as yours. Ours, our communication is through thought transference. All of you are quite capable of this though there are portions of your brain that are quite sluggish because of long disuse. But you shall be in our medical facility; you would be balanced; your frequency vibration would again be adjusted so that you would be comfortable.

You shall also receive classes, both individual and in small groups, for those of you that would be coming back to Earth after the cleansing period.

Your manner of clothing while with us would be -- how shall I say -- it would be a one piece suit. The men and the women's suits would basically be the same and it would be in a color that would be coded according to your specific purpose. I am sure, just as we do, you shall find these suits quite comfortable.

For your convenience we shall have specific meal times where ones of Earth might gather. Though I must say we are endeavoring to have many of your foods with which you are familiar, you shall find that there are a large number that shall seem quite different to you. I would urge you to partake of these for you shall find they are quite nutritious and have quite a lasting quality. These shall be foods that come from other planets, from other places within your universe. And some of the fruits you shall eat for the first time will be the ones that you shall find on Earth when you return.

You shall find that we have a beverage that at your first taste you would think of it as your earthly wine. No, this is not so. We serve no alcoholic beverages but you shall find this to be quite refreshing and relaxing.

Each of you, as I said, will have classes individually as well as in small groups with our beloved leaders, with the commanders within the Federation and with specific ones of the spiritual hierarchy. Here again this will be according to your purpose and what your role is in the days to come.

Many of you shall be returning to Earth for your role is to help to build the new Earth. Your role is to help to parent the seeds that will come forth. Others of you will have finished that which you have come to do and you shall be returning to your home planets, your home stars. You shall be returning to distant galaxies. And others shall be ascending to yet another dimension.

As I am sure you are aware, I feel such a joy to speak with you this evening. I have waited for this opportunity as I have been in service to the Radiant One. I eagerly await your arrival as do your other brothers and sisters...

The great room you spoke of, is there only one of these on the ship where everybody will be going or are there several?

ALEVA There is one great room that you will all be going to as you come into the ships. It is a large reception hall that all will be gathering. But in my haste, in my enthusiasm, I did not share with you the amphitheater which we have where there are meetings conducted. There are also small, smaller anterooms off the main recaption hall where groups might also gather. But initially there shall be one great room where those of the celestial hierarchy and those of us of the Confederation and those of you of Earth might gather initially to ease your transition into our dimension.

Now here I speak of the reception room on the mother ships. Some of you shall be coming up to smaller ships initially to be beamed to the mother ships, the command ships later. Now this later is a very short time, I assure you. In Earth terms it could be but a matter of moments, less than one hour of your earth time.

The ones we will meet in the great room, will some of them be our earthly relatives, friends that have passed on, our earthly acquaintances as well as our soul acquaintances?

ALEVA Yes, yes, yes, yes, yes, yes and won't it be joyful for we shall all be together and we shall recognize one another, and we shall all embrace in the universal and how joyous it will be!

I would urge you to do all within your capability within your present dimension to raise your vibratory rate for this shall hasten your transition with us and make it easier for you.

My dear brothers and sisters we are on the final countdown and such joy we have awaiting your arrival. When the hour comes it shan't be necessary for you to bring any of your would-be clothing with you. All that will be provided. All that you shall require will be in your room. Do not be concerned about taking anything with you.

Because this will be an evacuation phase much of the formality will be dispensed with because of the large numbers we shall be working with in a relatively short period of time...

ALEVA (shares more information about the ships) ...First and largest are our mother ships which would be likened to one of your cities such as your capital city, Washington B.C.-- excuse me, I believe I am in error, it is supposed to be D.C., correct? These are literally cities within the air. The next size is the command ships which might be likened to your football field size. Then there are the ships of the sector leaders which are slightly smaller. Then there is a variety of smaller ones down to the remote controlled scout ships.

In the time of lift-off all will be used to bring you up from Earth as quickly as possible. You will be sorted to the correct mother ships as you are beamed up.

I would add the key to the safe and expedient transition is to have no fear -- HAVE NO FEAR. We endeavor in our communiques to alleviate any fear that you might have. As we read the monitors we see many questions that pertain to your present state on Earth now. Some we are unable to answer because they will no longer be pertinent once you have joined us. So many things of earthly consequence now shall be relegated to the pile of trivia in the days to come. So my dear sister, this is the reason for many of man's unanswered questions.

Many of you are saying that you have not been in our ships. Not so. During the past five years most of you have spent much of your sleeping hours with us. It is just not time to activate your recall. Indeed when you come on board you will feel quite at home and quite familiar with your surroundings. Some of you in the days before you may begin to experience brief flashes of these sojourns. This will happen as we begin your activation...

I had heard that once we go up our bodies will be turned back to about 30 years old.

ALEVA This is so, and each of you -- well let me see what words shall I use for this -- you will not have an age. Each of you shall be quite youthful in appearance and vigor. There shall be no age here for we have no aging process as you have, but each of you shall be quite youthful, though I hesitate to give you a specific age, for really I am not quite familiar with your ages. That whole process to me is a puzzlement...

Could you tell us more about the classes we will be involved in?

ALEVA ...There are some of you on Earth at this time that will be teaching some of the classes here in the ships. No, you are not aware of it in your present dimension. But, once you have arrived here and you have become attuned you will find you have a great deal of wisdom that shall be released, wisdom that is needed to be shared with those that shall return to Earth.

Some of you may be teaching classes in healing. Some of you may be attending classes in healing, in balancing and what we would call the medical arts. Others shall be attending classes that they shall learn how to help others for soul advancement. In your earthly terms today these would be called your religious leaders, though I truly hesitate to use such a term for it is most inadequate. Others of you shall be attending classes on food preparation, on utilization of your thought processes, on building and how to use your basic materials that you will find once you return to Earth. Some of you will be attending classes on the flora and the fauna that you will find when you return. All of you will be receiving teaching from our most blessed ones. Various cosmic and universal laws will be shared with you and you will learn how to live with, to work with and to be in harmony with these laws.

Oh there is so much before you, there is so much, and how great it will be! Such joy there will be!

But as I said, to continue, many of you will be attending these various classes. These will not be large classes. They will probably be limited to 30 or 40 individuals at a time. Then, during the day there will be various gatherings within our amphitheater that will involve all of us that we might receive teachings, that we might receive guidance and instruction from the commanders within the Federation, as well as our beloved Sananda, our beloved Commander-in-Chief, and others of the celestial hierarchy may be coming to us to share lessons, to share of their knowledge and their experience.

I cannot give you specific time periods that these will happen. I cannot say to you how long each of you will be with us, within our ships, for I don't know. I do know that part of you ones of Earth shall be returning back to Earth, the builders, the pioneers, shall spend a brief time on another planet that you might learn to utilize some of your studies and your instructions, that you might be able to put into application the teachings that you have received. Here again you would have ones working with you most closely, for there shall be ones of the Fleet that shall be on this planet as well as returning to Earth with you to help you in your initial days there.

As I said, I cannot give you a specific time frame for this I do not know. I do know that you will be involved in a much greater variety of activities than you thought were possible. For all aspects of your soul development and evolvement shall be covered during your classes with us.

There shall be some of you, after you have completed your lessons or you have taught specific groups of lessons, that shall be going forth to your home planets. I am sure that as you become aware of your status that you will be most happy to return. And as you come aboard our ships messages, communiques, thoughts from loved ones, from your home stars and planets will await you. Also, it will be quite easy for you to send messages to them from our ships, much easier than it is from your present position on Earth, for we do not have the denseness that you all enjoy at this hour. Indeed, the messages shall literally fly through the ethers that you might enjoy a free communique...

ALEVA (in a later message, states) ...Everything is in readiness. Additional ones have come from the outer galaxy and from other galaxies. And at the present time our workload per individual one has been decreased so that we have more opportunity to talk with you, and to send forth energies to specific ones at specific groups that we might help each of you along you path.

I have been given additional assistance in working with your "big brothers and big sisters" should the time arise that you come aboard our ships. Indeed additional ones have come forth and are assuming roles so that our ratio of one to five has decreased and we are hoping that soon we shall be on a one to one ratio. This would be most lovely and would give each of you an individual escort in the days to come.

We have also been working with foodstuffs here within our ships so that we might have more foods that are more compatible with your digestive systems, as well as having the nutritive value that your physical beings need. We are aware that each of you needs a continued supply of protein in order to rebuild and to recharge the cellular structure of your bodies. Because we use only vegetable foodstuffs, our chefs are working most diligently to present these in a manner that shall be pleasing to the eye as well as the palate that you will not tire of these foods that we present to you. We have monitored and we watch most closely the dietary habits of you ones of Earth. I must say, as you come forth we shall be spending a good deal of time on proper nutrition, and the preparation of foods properly that you might get the maximum out of the foods that you intake. Oh there is so much that we have to share, and we are most anxious to share with you...

ALEVA ...I have, since I have last spoken with you, I have travelled to three distant stars that I might speak with others that are more informed, that are more advanced along their path than I.   For you see in some instances, I too, am still in school, though I assure you I am not in the same sort of school that you are in. I have travelled to these areas that I might become more familiar with these stars, with the actual landscape, with the cities, and with the ones that dwell there. So for you eartheans that might possibly travel to these distant stars, I feel that it would be most advantageous that I would be able to discuss these with you firsthand, so that you would have a bit of an orientation before you popped off there.

I shall in the upcoming days be taking visits to some of the other planets within this universe that I might familiarize myself with these, so that those of you that shall be going to these for brief sojourns, after your initial stay with us, that I might have more firsthand knowledge of these places, and that I might share this knowledge with those of you that are going, and also with others within the Fleet that have not had the opportunity to go to these planets before. For you see one of my primary jobs is to help to make each of you feel welcome and comfortable when you come on board with us. But also I do take the opportunity to share the information that I gather with other ones that are here on the ships that have not had the opportunity to travel to these other planets. So you see I stay quite busy.

Now I must take my leave of you. Blessings in the Light of the Radiant One, and my love I freely share with each of you, and to all that will read of my words in the distant day.   And to all of Earth mankind I send love that he might awaken, and that he might come forth to dwell with us. And, oh it shall be so beautiful when all of you of Earth know the peace that we know. Good night.

* * * * *

Salutations, Eartheans, Cuptan Fetogia speaking to you from that which is the Third Galaxy, and as the representative of the Inner Council Ring. I bring greetings to all ones of planet Earth. I bring love and encouragement to all Light bearers upon the planet.

I am advised that distant galaxies, universes, and dimensions are eagerly awaiting your return. Know, dear ones upon the planet that your reunion is assured. Hold fast to that thought form. Recognize that we hold you in great love. We salute you for that which you have come to do.

On behalf of all ones, know you are watched over and your steps are guided, if that is your choice.

I am Cuptan Fetogia signing off.

Salu Salu Salu

* * * * *

It has been our desire in this discussion to answer many of the questions you have regarding the intense periods for planet Earth and her peoples. We want you to know what to expect as you are brought upon the large ships. We want you to be in a state in which you have no fear, for fear immobilizes you and holds you bound. We desire for each of you to be free to be all you can Be.

Sarna, out.

THE NEW DAY

Greetings in the Light of the Radiant One. Sarna,here. The topic selected for this portion is that one of Earth, its inhabitants and the New Day. What a joyful topic it is! It is a topic which answers many of your questions. Your participants are Commanders Hatonn, Jokhym, Keilta, Beatrix, Soltec, Monka and I. We start with a question.

Could you share with us what it will be like on Earth in the beginning of the New Day?

HATONN Greetings, my brothers, my sisters. ...I would first say to you to search your memory for the meadow after the spring rain, and inhale its fragrance, and see the clarity, the beauty, the cleanliness that this washing has given to the grasses of the meadow. Do you remember the joy that filled your being at merely being there in that experience? Yes, I feel you do.

Earth's terrain shall not be as you know it this day for there is much that has been sleeping for this portion of the cycle that must come forth. And part of that which you know as the lands shall go beneath the surface of the waters to be washed, to be bathed, to be soothed. But those lands that many of you shall walk upon will have a rolling hill about them. You shall have your streams, your gentle lazy streams, that wind through your meadows. And there shall be the rivers. No, you will not see cities. You will not see hamlets. Initially, you will see the lands. And in some cases some of you might see the animals, those small folk that shall live with you in peace and harmony.

You will have received instruction, concentrated instruction on precipitation, on teleportation. As you come back to Earth many of us will come with you, to work with you, to assist you in forming structures, putting forth your seeds, and bringing forth your harvests. We shall assist you and teach you how to use the energy currents that flow about Earth that you might travel of these quite easily. We will share with you thought transference, telecommunication that you might be able to communicate with each other.

Small groups of you shall come together under the tutelage of one of us in various places about your Earth. Then as this group has grown sufficiently to be able to function independently the teacher shall remove themselves for a period to give them opportunity to "try their wings," so to speak.

You ones that will be with us, that will return to Earth, shall be highly developed individuals. You will be ones that have practiced and will practice all of the skills, all of the gifts that you have. And you will recognize these as gifts and as divine trusts, and treat them accordingly.

You will not have the severity of seasons in your locations that you presently have. So you will not be exposed to the extreme weather patterns that you now experience. There shall be grasses. There shall be flowers. And yes, there shall be trees that bear fruit. In many ways it shall be as is portrayed in your book of "Genesis", "In the beginning......". Thus, will be Earth in the new day. And we will work most closely as tutors, as brothers, as mentors to assist you to build the Perfect on planet Earth.

I saw a documentary on the Galapagos Islands, where we saw the animal life not afraid of man, in fact, even curious about man. In the future how will the relation with man and the animal life be since man will be going on the fourth dimension and the animal life, I suppose, will be staying on the third dimension?

JOKHYM In the radiance of the Source, I greet you. ...Your observation of this particular place upon your planet is indeed a good one. However, there is one small, small inaccuracy in that which you say, in that the animal will not stay on the third plane, but the animal, too, will go with you as you rise in consciousness. Indeed, there are animals, that which you would call the small ones that are entrusted to you, that are already being prepared for that which is your new Earth, and there shall be a great communion. Indeed, it shall be as it was intended, as it was of a distant day, when ones would speak to these, the ones that were within their charge, and they would work with you and they would serve with you in a harmonious manner. For there was no intent to enslave that which is your beasts, your creatures of your field. There was no intent that this would be, but rather, that this would be a communion, a sharing in abilities.

Those which were fleet of foot would willingly carry you upon their backs where you would desire to go, until such time as you can go without the aid of transport of your being. And these ones that would be the flesh-eating ones upon your plane are being removed that there would be only those that would live in a harmonious way.

There is a great communion, there is a trust that is established with you and the creature of the field. If you will accept that -- and this shall come into being in that which is considered your new day -- indeed, there are those of you now that will note that your energy patterns have altered sufficiently that there are small four-legged ones that will come to you in great comfort, have you not? Have you not had the bird come close to you -- the small ones would come and they would sing their sweet songs to you. For indeed, there was of a distant day that which was the temple chorus and it was the song of the bird. And they would gather at that which was the rising of your sun, and their song would be that of beautiful greeting. And then as their sun would go to rest or to sleep, they would gather once again and they would sing the lullaby to you to prepare you for your slumber. And again, this shall come to be. And they will come together of many kinds that there will be a great chorus for you.

And there shall be others that would willingly let you place your head upon their back, for they would desire to be close to you. For you must remember, you represent the God essence. There is that which is the divine essence within you that attracts these ones, and it is that trust of the attraction that you have lost in this process that you have experienced that you will again reclaim.

In the Bible it says that the lambs will eat with the lions. Is this to be taken literally or metaphorically?

JOKHYM You may take it as you would choose, but it shall be in fact. For the lion shall no longer be that which is the flesh-eating eater, but the lion will be content to graze and to eat of the vegetation, even as does the lamb. So, there is that which is the metaphor that is given to you, and there is also that which is the truth of the moment. So it may be taken in several ways. For it does mean that that which is the power will come into balance with that which is the meek.

Will planet Earth ever have one language?

SARNA Oh yes, my brother, yes. There shall be one language. There shall be one blending of energies as each one is allowed to grow along their path, and are respected in that which they do. As Earth evolves and those evolve with her, language shall no longer be necessary. But thought transference shall be the rule, and this is a common transference that is understood regardless of where you are or what your experiences are. This shall be most delightful, and it shall be most gratifying that we will be able to also share our thoughts with all ones of Earth, and they shall knowingly receive them -- just as one will share in the thoughts of their brother.

Will our mode of education be different than it is now?

BEATRIX Greetings, beloveds. ...My dear beloved one, I would hope that your system would change radically, for that system which you are now experiencing is older than archaic -- if there is such a term. Your educational system has been established to bring about the maximum of conformity, with the minimum of effort to induce the conformity. And this has been done under the guise of giving you freedom to learn and express yourselves.

Some of you, as you travel back through your experiences before this embodiment, will recall some of the education that you have experienced on Helox (a planet with a universal university). Just as no two entities are exactly alike, how can we begin to attempt to educate -- and here that is an incorrect word also -- how can we help ones to grow in their own development and their awareness if we try to do everyone the same way? Each of you has your own pattern of growth. Each of you has your own particular mode of growth, your own area of specialization, your own pattern of thought transference, and your own degree of awareness. The educational process is to allow you, to encourage you, to challenge you to evolve to your maximum potential at a specific period. In observing your educational system I would say this approach is sadly lacking.

Know, dear one, you shall find that the educational system in the distant day -- which is much closer than you realize -- shall not be of the same type that you are presently experiencing. Those of you that recall Socrates, and those that are known as the Greek scholars, will recall the method of teaching that was done at that time; that one was challenged to think, not to become a mechanical robot that regurgitates back specific thoughts, but one was taught to think, to expand their own awareness. This is the main, the primary objective of an educational process is to allow each one to grow at their own particular rate that they would seek of truth, and as truth is revealed to them that they would strive always for a greater, deeper truth. This, the educational process shall bring forth.

May we say those things which you now are experiencing are most superfluous, and are quite unnecessary to that which you have come to do. Though I recognize at this hour you cannot change your educational process, for those that are in the leadership positions would not understand what you are attempting to do, know that in the day that is the New Day, the process which you now have will be dissolved, that the one of allowing the individual, encouraging the individual to evolve and to grow, and to question, and to seek within themselves shall be the rule and not the exception.

Will there be an introduction of new grains with more protein in them as a substitute for meat?

KEILTA Greetings, dear ones of planet Earth. ...There are many new grains, there are new commodities -- and I use this as a collective term, for you on planet Earth -- that shall be coming into your awareness, for they have been introduced to the planet already...

I am aware that many of you are now repulsed by the thought of eating red meat, for you recognize how this was grown, why this was grown, and the life that was given to this animal, and the amount of fear that this animal has had that is conveyed into the products that are made from it. As man's vibratory frequency is elevated he has less and less need for this, and he seeks other methods of feeding his vehicle. Indeed, when man reaches this state, then foodstuffs are provided for him that will nourish him and assist him in maintaining his vehicle in that vibratory frequency.

Could you talk to us about potential energy sources that might be used in future days? For example, does the

mobeus loop have anything to do with the process of obtaining free energy?

BEATRIX ...Indeed, that which you speak is better known in other realms than it is upon your own. There is an energy pattern that is established within this loop, and as specific points are brought together within the loop there is a commonality that accelerates and magnifies the energy flow that is existent within the loop. In the days ahead, there shall be a careful study of this method of energy convergence, for there is a commonality of points within this that shall bring about an energy acceleration for those that are working with it.

You upon your planet in many instances do not recognize the resources that you have available to you that do not cost your dollars and cents. You do not recognize the fact that by working with the ley lines of your planet, and bringing about an alignment with your polar regions that you can set up a force field that will indeed bring electrical power to you. This loop is another example of how energy can be harnessed in a simple manner merely by altering the pattern of specific lines to produce a greater magnetic attraction in the field of commonality to bring about a greater energy source for you. I have not gone into great detail but have merely touched the tip of the iceberg that I might answer your question.

SOLTEC Greetings and salutations. ...With the combination of the correct chemical composition you can place a pole, a stick, in the ground, and from that you can have energy for all of your uses within your home. You can do this, also, with the energies from your sun. There have been some inroads made into that...

While on Earth, Nikola Tesla tapped into an unknown cosmic energy and drove a "fuelless" car that went over

100 miles an hour. Would you comment on this?

SARNA ...Indeed, as you proceed within this next thousand year period, you will see great changes in the transportation systems upon your planet. For you shall have conveyances that do not have wheels, but ride along a path of air, a cushion of energy; that they might be controlled by thought patterns to take you wherever you would choose to go upon your planet.

That one, this beautiful one that is with us (Tesla), indeed was given, exposed to Earth man many of the -- and I hesitate to use the word inventions, for indeed, this is such an archaic term -- but he shared with you many thought manifestations that were beyond the acceptability level of those that were embodied during his period. But he planted a seed. And this is what he came to do. He planted a seed with many ones. And this seed is not dormant, but it is growing within a wide group as interests are awakened, and one begins to tap into the meaning, the understanding, the awareness of what was involved in these thought manifestations that he brought forth.

So there shall be a conveyance that will go as the wind. And there will be conveyances that will take you to other planets as well. But then these shall seem quite archaic to you when you shall be able to leave of one form to take form on another planet, that you will need no conveyance for you will have the ability within yourself to do this. But, the conveyances shall be used in the interim until you have polished your skills sufficiently to make these trips on your own.

Will some of the ancient records be revealed to us in the future times?

MONKA Blessings in the Light of the most Radiant One. ...Much shall be coming to your attention in the upcoming days. Information shall become available to you ones of Earth in the near future that has not been available before. You are approaching that point in the cycle when records that have long been buried and concealed shall be revealed. You are approaching that point in your cycle when you shall see the original writings as they were made. You shall become aware of their preservation, and how they were preserved. And you shall become aware of that which they foretold on that long distant day.

The time is approaching, as the three cycles come to a close, that there shall be a great rendering of Earth. And just as your Book of Revelations, in your most Holy Book, has given you a pictorial view of that which shall happen, so it is now as the cycles close that that which was foretold shall come into being...

The records that you speak of, is this something other than the Dead Sea Scrolls?

HATONN Oh yes, oh yes, these records that our brother speaks of are ones that go far beyond those that are known to you as the Dead Sea Scrolls. These are records that were buried long before the time that there is recorded history upon your planet, for these are records of the distant days of Lemuria, and of certain times within the cycle of Atlantis.

Each one of these civilizations has specific gifts that they brought forth, and in the foreseeable future -- and here again I ask your indulgence, for I give you not day, time or place -- but these records shall come to the forefront. And those that are capable of holding the trust shall have the mystery of these records revealed to them.

Will this include access to the emerald tablets of Hermes?

SARNA This shall not come forth in your immediate future.

But there shall be a period after that which is called your period of tribulation that more of these shall be revealed. And indeed, there shall come forth ones that will carry these tablets, that they will be as teachers or guides to assist in the awakening process of others. But this shall not be done until such time as there is a band that has been well prepared and is strong within their core and within their inner beings, individually and collectively, before this is done.

* * * * *

Let all of us look forward to that place in the grand cycle when Earth man may be at peace with himself, with his brothers, with the animals of the field, the fishes of the sea, and the birds of the air as well as the planet of Earth.

Sarna, out.

MAY PEACE AND LOVE PREVAIL
UPON THE EARTH

Salutations Eartheons. I am Cuptan Fetogia. Greetings in the Light of the Eternal Principle. My message is the message of all Fetogia: Peace, Love, Peace, Love.

You Eartheons are on a most tenuous step. You at this hour might easily falter and possibly fail. The leaders of your planet must come together in peace and brotherhood for all of the planet. The present approach your countries are taking with one another is most devastating and will lead to eventual annihilation if you are allowed to continue on your present approach. Fortunately for all souls involved with Earth, the Councils and Confederation will not let your leaders continue to that point.

My message is to all of Earth: <u>Lay down your weapons; lay down your arms; defuse your bombs and silence your satellites</u>. This is the only approach that will have lasting positive consequences. Your conscious implementation of these steps will save you from an irrevocable path of destruction.

Eartheons, hear my words. I, Cuptan Fetogia, have seen ones similar to you destroy their cosmic base. These ones have suffered untold scarring and sorrow. Do not make the same mistake in trying to duplicate what has been done. Your time shortens. Your time shortens. Do not allow your leaders, your ones in positions of responsibility to act in an emotional frenzy. Do not allow these ones to propel you into a situation that might have devastating effects upon the souls of all ones attached to the planet Earth.

To you ones of the Light Forces, go forth that the Light might be shared with all. Know what you are, and stand firm in who you are. I salute you each one. All ones of Fetogia send blessings and salutations to all ones of Earth. Their love they share freely with all ones of Light.

I shall close this communique.

Salu Salu Salu

* * * * *

Let peace prevail upon Earth. I speak with one thought, one voice from within the Cosmos. I speak as the Ashtar Command. I speak as the voice of the Masters of Knowing and the Great White Brotherhood. I am the Christ and the thought that originates from within the Source. Let peace prevail upon the Earth.

The hour of separation is lost to that which is the moment of coming together. Let all ones join in one thought form. As the Christed energies intensify within each of you, the peoples of Earth, let the joining in Oneness be manifested.

You who call yourselves the leaders of this new age of enLIGHTenment come together as equals in the Christ Body. You who seek of the treasures and the reclamation of the beauty of the Earth Mother, come join with these ones. Let no separation be within those ones that would call themselves of the Light. Let no differences demonstrate, but see of the similarities.

You who would be as the communicators of our words to planetary man, join hands with one another. See of the portion that is given through you as just what it is, a portion, to be put together with the others. Let the bells peal of the oneness. Let silence be the signal of separateness.

You who claim of your service and your dedication, the hour is when you have the ability to demonstrate this. Come, join hands and sing the Hosannas... May, all ones who desire of a serious desire know they shall be initiated into the realm of their origin. Yea, if ye be Light then so shall

194

ye be Light evermore! Let this be the knowing that shall walk of the face of the Earth Mother. Let this be the knowing for all mans kind.

Planetary shifting and alignment is occurring which is beyond the comprehension of mere mortal form. Truly the forces of the Divine come to add their voice to yours in the rejoicing. May each who do commit to the step of acceleration, know there is no returning to the ordinary, the norm, the mere state of mortal limitation. Examine of your commitment. Search deep within your innermost heart that you would know of your purpose and your reason for being. May the Christ within each come forth to join with the Christ within your brother. May those who would choose the path of lethargy, be as ones blest in their sleep.

Man has put forth the call for assistance, for his deliverance. Yet, he is as one to see of his own portion as that which is the receiver. I say to all mans kind, even as you receive so it is that you shall give to all others. Lay aside your differences and see of your oneness.

The councils do come together and the Elders do ponder of the state of mans kind of the Emerauld. Let no man be as one to sleep, let each reach up to his golden seed beginning. Feel of the acceleration as the old gives way to the new. It is that the concepts that held man captive shall be washed from the consciousness leaving a cleanness for that which is the new.

Informations, concepts, knowledge shall come into the awareness of the Earth man that shall be as the greatest rocking of the Earth's surface. The gates have been opened. The eyes unveiled. Those who would take the step through this blessed portal shall be the Light manifested.

Release all that is the acceptance of limitation. Accept no limitation of thought or form. Begin to experience this so that you might take the rapid acceleration... None shall be omitted. None shall be caught napping. Each shall have of their own opportunity to make their commitment before the

Elders of Light. Even as the commitment is made so it is each is then given what is necessary to manifest the Light that is theirs.

In the twelfth month of your calendar year that is 1988, the Elders of Light put forth the call. You have completed of a troublesome period, one of cleansing and acknowledgment. You have now to come forth through the cleansing of the waters of initiation to be the born Christ Light. Rejoice! Rejoice! Let no man of the planet sleep a dreamless sleep. Awaken! Awaken! Your hour of birth is with you. Changing starts. Orbiting planets, galaxies of brotherhood all align in readiness for this moment, this now. Know of your portion, prepare to bring it forth. Cast from yourselves all that is not of your Christed Order.

I AM COME TO AWAKEN WITHIN ALL MANS KIND THE DIVINITY THAT IS THEIR ORIGIN. Unlock your hearts. See of the assistance that is given forth. Be of that assistance as you hold forth the hand to your brothers. Let no man fall because of weariness, but let another lift him that the way might be made together.

I am the voice that heralds of that which shall be. I am the voice of comfort for all ones along the way. I am the voice that leads of the column as it ascends to the mountain top. I am the receiver as each comes to their pinnacle. I AM the Christ within each and I AM the Christ that awaits to be fulfilled. I AUM.

* * * * *

We now close this small volume. The seal is placed upon this volume as it is placed upon the ones before it. Glean from this book that which is of succor and assistance to nurture you along your pathe.

My beloved brethren upon planet Earth, on behalf of all ones of the realms beyond your own, I speak to you to begin your pathe of ascension. Raise up from the vibration of materialism, self-centeredness, and isolation. See of the commonality which resides in the hearts of each of you rather than the differences of ethnic, color, race, place or class. Lift up your voices in oneness to be the clarion call for brotherhood.

It is you who lay the foundation for the new Jerusalem. It is you who hold the mantle which allows for the change. Let no man take from you the divine right of your being. As you acknowledge of your own divinity so it is that a bonding and strengthening of bonding welds you with your brethren of the realms beyond that which you call your reality.

I Aum Cum. Announce My arrival by your own example, for it is that you lay the foundation, the pavement for Me. We are in oneness, you and I -- brother with brother who brings forth the New Day.

I Aum Sananda.

Publications by

Portals of Light, Inc.

Talks With The Masters: Theoaphylos

Talks With The Masters: El Morya

Talks With The Masters: Serapis Bey

Letters From Home: Vol. I

Letters From Home: Vol. II

Letters From Home: Vol. III

Letters From Home: Vol. IV

Conclave: Meeting Of The Ones

Conclave: 2nd Meeting

Conclave: 3rd Meeting

Conclave: 4th Meeting

Hello, I'm Tobias. Can I come Talk To You?